stiletto

caroline cox

stiletto

MITCHELL BEAZLEY

Stiletto

Caroline Cox

First published in 2004 by Mitchell Beazley,
an imprint of Octopus Publishing Group Ltd,
2–4 Heron Quays, London E14 4JP

ISBN 1 84000 906 3

A CIP catalogue copy of this book is available
from the British Library

Commissioning Editor: Mark Fletcher
Executive Art Editor: Sarah Rock
Managing Editor: Hannah Barnes-Murphy
Project Editor: Emily Asquith
Designers: Fiona Pike and Alexa Brommer
Production Controller: Gary Hayes

Set in Scotch Roman and Veljovic

To order this book as a gift or an incentive contact
Mitchell Beazley on 020 7531 8481

Printed and bound in China by
Toppan Printing Company Limited

page 2 *Illustrator Francis Marshall
captures the allure of the* haute couture
*salon show in the early 1950s.
The stiletto made one of its first
appearances at the House of Dior.*

page 5 *A stiletto designed in 2004
by Sandra Choi for Jimmy Choo,
a sought-after label with an enviable
celebrity client list that specializes
in expensive luxury heels.*

contents

"Most women prefer to trip to hell in high heels than to walk flat-heeled to heaven." [i]

The stiletto spells sex. Its spiked heel has erotic allure and is a supreme symbol of femininity. Invented in the 1950s by Italian shoemakers, the spindle-heeled stiletto was assertively modern, releasing women from the utilitarian fashions of the wartime 1940s and launching them into a modern era of fashionable consumption. The precision-engineered shape of the original heel continued to be developed on the Continent until the weight of the body could be balanced on an area no bigger than a dime. Stilettos became a global phenomenon, revered and reviled across the world. In Europe and the United States women wore the tapered or "needle heel," as early stilettos were dubbed, and in Hong Kong the stiletto heel was known as the "five-cent," after the heel tip, which was no bigger than a Hong Kong nickel. By the early 1960s fashion mavens sought the slimmest possible stiletto heel, by then produced using techniques borrowed from the towering architectural form of the skyscraper, where metal girders were placed in concrete shells for maximum support. The piercing, penetrating nature of the heel caused disturbance wherever it roamed, damaging floors and in some cases the feet of others, sparking outrage and moral panic. The fact that the bottom tips needed regular replacement spawned a new kind of business: the heel bar. Doctors condemned women wearers for damaging their feet, backs, and posture.

Of course heels existed before the invention of the stiletto and the highest heels have always walked a delicate tightrope between the elegant and the vulgar, with those prepared to wear them seen as worldly or just plain stupid. As shoe historian Mary Trasko succinctly puts it, "wherever heels have marched across the map of history they seem to have produced a ripple of nervous and slightly scandalized reaction." [2] Created in the sixteenth century for reasons of military utility and status, heels were useful for men as stirrup holders on riding boots and to control the horse during rough riding. But as anthropologist Margaret Visser points out, "their first purpose was to raise their owners, enable them to pose impressively, and stretch their legs so that their calf muscles bulged curvaceously out." [iii] By the eighteenth century, heels had become court wear for women – a mark of conspicuous leisure – and so representative of the social hierarchy of the culture of the time. The celebrated sexologist Richard von Kraft-Ebbing made just this point in 1886: "The hierarchical principle governs not only predilection for smallness of foot, but also the desire literally and symbolically to lift it out of the mud, with high heels raising the woman visually above the common herd and at the same time suggesting that walking is a special and difficult, rather than commonplace activity for her." [iv] Fashion historian Quentin Bell agrees, calling high heels "the most effectual guarantee of social standing." [v] They were also very much about glamorous allure, but equally evoked ridicule and contempt. Fashion historian Colin MacDowell describes how in the eighteenth century,

"a wag made fun of the tyranny of high heels with his couplet addressed to fashion victims: 'Mount on French heels when you go to a ball, It now is the fashion to totter and fall.' And indeed at the court of Louis XVI, women wore such extreme high heels that they could walk only with the aid of a stick and could not tackle stairs without the help of an admirer, servant, or, if all else failed, a husband. The female high heel was curved and tilted to make women look provocative – in much the same way as high heels do today." [vi]

In the twentieth century it has become conventional for women to wear high heels and unnatural for men, considered more suited to the drag act or the fetishist's closet. High heels have been incorporated so successfully into feminine culture that it is only when dressing as women that men can wear them. Even then, for some male renegades stiletto heels have been important markers of outlaw culture and rage against the establishment. One prime example is the infamous Stonewall riots in 1969 where feisty drag queens were heard chanting to police, "We are the Stonewall girls – we wear our hair in curls; we wear no underwear; we show our pubic hair," as they went on the attack brandishing their heels.

The stiletto is the high heel in its most extreme, modern, and dangerous form. There's even a surface missile named after it, the Raytheon Stiletto, which makes the association between death and the piercing quality of the stiletto knife and shoe. Not for nothing do we refer to a

opposite *Throughout the 1960s British artist Allen Jones played with the stiletto as a fetish symbol in his Pop Art imagery, constantly reworking the idea of the dominatrix in latex and high heels.*

pair of stilettos as killer heels. These are shoes that blatantly contravene the original purpose of footwear, to protect the feet and aid mobility – stilettos are pretty uncomfortable, even painful, after a hard night of partying. Contemporary philosopher Marcel Danesi wrote in 1999, "If I watched people as one might observe animals in their natural habitats, one would soon reach the conclusion that human beings are truly a peculiarity. Why is it that some females of the same species make locomotion a struggle for themselves by donning high-heel footwear?" [vii]

So why do millions of women choose to wear them? This book will attempt to uncover the lure of the needle heel. The first chapter, Fancy Footwork, charts the development of the stiletto heel and the prime movers in its development, its position at the heart of Parisian couture, and the new demands of consumption that were made on the 1950s housewife. The stiletto was seen to be a new symbol of postwar modernity – classy, elegant, and high fashion. By the decade's end, as the second chapter, Hollywood Heels, demonstrates, the image of the stiletto had changed. Overtly sexy Hollywood stars such as Marilyn Monroe and Jayne Mansfield wore stilettos, and the stiletto heel had become a recognizable weapon in the arsenal of female sartorial power, worn by both career-driven go-getters and "bad girls." The spiked heel symbolically freed them from the domesticated femininity of the basic court shoe and they were proud to sport the stiletto at its most defiantly extreme in the form of the winklepicker. High spiked heels spelled danger – even the name was derived from a knife, the stiletto traditionally being a stealthy and dangerous blade favoured first by Renaissance assassins and later by the criminal underbelly of Sicily. It is this association of sex and death that makes the stiletto so compelling, and the prime reason for its status as fetish object is explained in full in the third chapter, Spikes and Lashes. This chapter also assesses the problematical gender politics of the stiletto heel. Does it enslave or promote power in women? Odalisques in the harem of Turkish sultans, for instance, were forced to wear precarious high heels to stop them running off, and the Chinese bound foot caused intense pain, yet gains in return included increased social status and socialized beauty. Vestiges of this attitude can be found in the late 1950s winklepicker shoe. The payoff for the stiletto wearer is increased height and a kind of super-femininity. At 10–12 centimetres (4–5 inches) it cancels out any height difference between the sexes, and in some instances has been used as a weapon with devastating results. Journalist Shoshana Goldberg cites the case of a New York woman in 2003 "who beat her ex-boyfriend to death with her high-heeled shoe outside a nightclub in Brooklyn. The fifty-year-old woman knocked him down and then struck him repeatedly with her shoe. The woman was charged with manslaughter and criminal possession of a weapon – her shoes." [viii]

The power of the stiletto is also made manifest in, thankfully, a less forceful way by many popular female icons. This power is linked to the fact that it is still in some ways culturally unacceptable for a woman to be taller than her husband. As psychologist Rita Freedman explains, "Size and strength influence social power....The diamorphism in size places females in the deferential position of looking up to males as an inferior looks up to a superior or as a child looks up to an adult. To stand above confers an inherent power advantage. Big females and little males are socially mismatched." [ix] Women are supposed to go for "tall, dark, and handsome" with the emphasis on tall and those whose husbands are shorter tend to wear flats. Although they were nearly equal in height, for their engagement photos in 1981 Prince Charles stood one step above Lady Diana Spencer to create the illusion of being the dominant male. Subsequently, after her split from the Royal Family, Princess Diana cut a striking silhouette by appearing in all the right places in her towering Jimmy Choos, a powerful woman in her own right no longer having to defer to her significantly shorter other. Actress Nicole Kidman made it clear she was still a force to be reckoned with after her divorce from Tom Cruise in 2001 by announcing she could now wear high heels – Cruise of course was also noticeably shorter. For both women, the choice of skyscraper stilettos was to give them a psychological advantage; they were noticeably "walking taller." However, as Rita Freedman goes on to point out, "fashions that confer the power of added size nearly always inhibit movement. A gain in the hedonic power of display is generally offset by a loss in the agonic power to act." [x] A woman in stiletto heels may appear powerful and dominating, but she can't do much more than stand there looking provocative. It is precisely this aspect of the stiletto that has proved to be an obsession for many writers, artists, and illustrators from the 1930s through to the 1970s. For many men it has been a fully-fledged obsession,

BOTTEGA VENETA

LONDON PARIS MILANO ROMA VENEZIA FIRENZE www.bvlux.com

opposite *Bottega Veneta, a Milan-based company famous for its luxury leather accessories, is part of the Gucci group. Under creative director Tomas Maier, the company produces cutting-edge stiletto designs.*

particularly when combined with the most extreme tight-laced corset. In this armoured garb, the high-heeled *femme fatale* such as Cruella DeVil from *101 Dalmations* cuts a spectacular figure. Punk women used precisely this language of sado-masochism and the rapier heel to invent a powerful femininity, which was to resurface in the "girl power" movement of the 1990s, as documented in the final chapter, Balancing Act.

Nowadays the stiletto has emerged as a high-fashion must-have. Despite being condemned by radical feminists as being an example of how women have crippled themselves in their quest for the fashionable ideal, by the twenty-first century the stiletto has regained its correct place in the hierarchy of feminine footwear and become a badge of status, authority, and sex appeal. So-called "limousine shoes" are no longer just high heels worn by those who paid others to walk for them, but are worn by women from every walk of life on every occasion. Designed by the likes of Manolo Blahnik, Jimmy Choo, Gina, Prada, and Gucci, stilettos are the badge of the fashion *cognoscenti* rather than the fashion victim. Men have always responded to the stiletto, too, either as designers (most are male) or as observers. As anthropologist Margaret Visser notes, "It has forever been the male habit when sizing up the physical attributes of the woman for his eye to start at the bottom with her feet and shoes, and gradually move up the body column. Women have always known this. This is why they have such a loyal affection for high heels, so that the male eye gets off to an encouraging start and has reason to complete the bottom-to-top visual tour with admiration." [xi]

Thus the meaning of the stiletto depends on its cultural context: a badge of rebellious liberation worn by an assertive modern woman; an overtly sexual emblem of woman as dominatrix; a shackling device to keep women both physically and mentally restrained; an object of desire enthusiastically embraced by Hollywood starlets; or an image vociferously reviled by radical feminists in the 1970s. This book will investigate these very issues using imagery and examples from a wide range of cultural and historical sources from the 1950s to the modern day, exploring the stiletto's long-term relationship with sex, femininity, fetishism, and female power. As the playwright George Bernard Shaw remarked, "If you rebel against high-heeled shoes, take care to do so in a very smart hat." [xi]

FANCY FOOTWORK

"The girl with low and sensible heels

Is likely to pay for her bed and meals."

Anon., 1950s

T he stiletto heel is a fantasy made real. Many dreamed of it yet few could realize it, and even now its exact origins are shrouded in mystery – which is surprising for a design of such sublimity. High heels had been a firm fashion favourite in the pre-war years, invoking a Hollywood glamour for women keen to escape the pressures of the Depression era. Copying the feminine, floaty styles of such stars as Carol Lombard and Ginger Rogers, women high-stepped into the 1940s until the logic of fashion and the restrictions of war demanded a change. Utility shoes, spearheaded by the wedge heel designs of Italian shoe master Salvatore Ferragamo (1898–1960), dominated the 1940s until even the designer himself was desperate for a transformation. For Ferragamo the typical 1940s shoe was "heavy [and] graceless … with points shaped like potatoes and heels like lead." [i] The famed editor of American *Vogue* Diana Vreeland (1906–89) also remembered shoes of that decade with antipathy,

"Everyone was in wooden shoes, *clack clack clack*. You could tell the time of day by the sound of the wooden soles on the pavement. If there was a great storm of them, it meant that it was lunch hour and people were leaving their offices for the restaurants. Then there would be another great clatter when they returned." [ii]

The chunkiness of the 1940s shoe was also due to limited technology, which meant that the verticality of its heel was constrained. Heels were made of a central core of wood which was then covered with leather and precluded any degree of taper – the thinner the wooden heel the more likelihood there was of breakage. This, together with a puritan streak that had, of necessity, entered fashion owing to the rigours of war, meant that glamour and ornament were eschewed in favour of comfort and practicality. A sensible, hard-wearing wool suit was the order of the day for a woman who had to cope with the rigours of rationing – an economy of dress to reflect the economy brought to bear on her domestic life. However, at the beginning of the 1950s, a new sound of the city could be heard, the infinitely

more seductive *click click click* of the high-heeled shoe. Ferragamo's fantasy designs in gold kid covered in satin butterfly wings and pink glass beading were a tonic to women who had been deprived of glamour during the war years and who hungered for a more romantic form of dressing. As journalist Ann Scott-James put it in her book *In the Mink*,

"As the last guns rumbled and the last all-clear sounded, all the squalor and discomfort and roughness that had seemed fitting for so long began to feel old fashioned … I wanted to throw the dried eggs out of the window, burn my shabby curtains, and wear a Paris hat again. The Amazons, the women in trousers, the good comrades, had had their glorious day. But it was over. Gracious Living beckoned once again." [iii]

By 1948 the British trade magazine *Footwear* had declared, "The heavy, bulky shoe is definitely OUT." [iv] Shoe manufacturers realized that they needed to respond rapidly to the new decade of affluence by making a shoe that could stimulate demand after the wartime stagnation of fashion, creating a whole new generation of female consumers. Women wanted new ideas and new looks after the gloom and rationing of the 1940s. The race was on – who could create an elegant, modernist shoe, one fitting for a new age and the expectations women had of fashion that had lain dormant for so long?

Postwar governments across the globe were persuading women back to the home and hearth, re-emphasizing their role in family life as nurturers and mothers, in what design historian Penny Sparke has described as a "re-energized domestification" [v] of women. A fear of a declining population after the rigours of war and a concomitant need for social stability led to an emphasis on the idea of the domesticated, child-bearing housewife – almost a reincarnation of religious poet Coventry Patmore's model of nineteenth-century femininity in his poem "The Angel in the House." [vi] Women who had been juggling work and family life during the 1940s were now being encouraged to abandon the competitive arena for the domestic and to devote themselves entirely to their husbands. As beauty writer Veronica Dengel observed in her book *Can I Hold My Beauty* (1946),

"The future of society and of the world can be improved in direct ratio to the manner in which the woman of today works to improve the unity of her home and family … Her efforts must be directed towards the cultivation of harmony, happiness, and peace in her home life. Only then can we hope for permanent peace in the world." [vii]

Housewifery was being sold through the mass media as a science, and the market was energetically directing products at the Happy Housewife – new washing machines, vacuum cleaners, even Tupperware. Wipe-clean surfaces and a happy life in the suburbs were the order of the day. But women also had to look good for their men – by day you may have been a domestic goddess, but at night you could transform yourself deliciously with the new feminine fashions. British writer Sue Townsend describes this almost schizophrenic existence

"Inside the house, most women slopped around in slippers, old clothes, and wraparound aprons … But after the house was cleaned a miracle would occur. A woman would retire to her bedroom [and] emerge as Grace Kelly … She wore stockings, suspenders, high heels, and a cinch-waisted frock … she smelt of Evening of Paris." [viii]

The cinch-waisted frock and high heels of this ubiquitous 1950s look derived in the main from French *haute couture* which for most of the pre-war era had provided the blueprint for a woman who wanted to dress up. Late 1940s and early 1950s styles began to re-emphasize the traditional female figure that had been lost with the rather masculinized wide-shouldered shape of the 1940s, "that seemed to have been created to support badges at rank or rifles at the slope," [ix] as British journalist Pearson Philips puts it. Skirts had been knee-length and jackets long, which, together with the wedge shoe and thick ankle straps,

had made the legs look short and rather ungainly. Women were ready for a new look, a more sexualized form that emphasized the bust, waist, and hips. They were prepared to embrace a traditionally feminine figure, which highlighted the sexual zones of a woman's body while at the same time, with its round-shouldered silhouette, had an air of submissiveness about it.

The signs had been there in 1945 when one hopeful fashion journalist had written in *Harper's Bazaar*, "this year brings a new era and it follows as the peace the war, that men want women beautiful, romantic birds of paradise instead of hurrying brown hens." [x] These were prophetic words, for in 1947 Christian Dior (1905–57) unveiled his New Look to an aghast but enraptured press. The look was of a haughty high-class femininity – tight tailoring, wasp waists, and huge crinoline skirts that mocked wartime sobriety and its attendant restrictions on the use of materials. When the "Corolle" line, as it was originally called, was shown to the assembled journalists, it entered the annals of fashion as a defining moment:

"The long frothy skirts of Dior's collection were so full that they brushed against the cheeks of the assembled crowd … The audience was shocked, enraptured, and captivated. Seasoned fashion journalists to this day remember that show as one of the most magical moments of their lives. Perhaps the huge quantity of Dior perfume that was sprayed over each member of the audience … made everyone a little light-headed." [xi]

This swelling, opulent look was for Janey Ironside, later to become Professor of Fashion at London's Royal College of Art, "like a new love affair, the first sight of Venice, a new chance, in fact a new look at life." [xii] Dior held "a mirror up to women, in which they saw themselves as they wished to be; no longer Amazons but Nymphs; no longer Cinders but Cinderella." [xiii]

The newly tightened waist, fitted bodice, padded hips, and bouffant skirts of Dior's New Look needed an accompanying shoe that complemented this new

above *A pair of silver stilettos with a winklepicker toe. The ruched front is lifted from the successful designs of Roger Vivier for Dior; this became a popular design motif in shoes made throughout the 1950s.*

right *High-fashion stilettos worn with the ubiquitous bouffant skirt, as photographed by John French in 1957; this frothy confection was inspired by Christian Dior's New Look of ten years earlier.*

frothy version of femininity. Utility styles were out as they were too heavy, thick-heeled, and functional, "with straps round ankles like footballer's laces" xiv – something new was needed. Footwear manufacturers debated "whether heels should reach a new extremity of height or a new low; which is the most flattering line for the ankle and interprets best the revival of flourishing femininity." xv

Step forward Parisian shoe designer Roger Vivier (1913–98), who was to become pivotal in the popularization of the newly tapered heel. Vivier worked with Spanish shoemaker Manuel Mantilla, who declared, "The foot is a southern speciality," xvi and Italian shoemaker Marguerite Gugliotta, "who sewed tiny strips of leather with deft fingers." xvii Vivier, in his customary shirt sleeves and red braces, created designs that were pure *haute couture*: classy, elegant, and exclusive, beloved by stars such as Grace Kelly. Known as the "Fabergé of Footwear," at the age of 17 Vivier worked on the floor of a small shoe factory which, as he put it, gave him the advantage of "being able to discover the basics empirically, forms that are as old as the world itself, which I subsequently combined and presented in my own way." xviii This practical start, together with his later training as a sculptor (he studied at the Ecole des Beaux-Arts in Paris), gave Vivier a unique combination of aesthetic and technical skills and made him perfectly placed to develop one of the prototype tapered heels for the newly rising couturier Dior in the early 1950s.

Working at Dior's side, Vivier designed shoes that perfectly complemented the romantic historicized silhouettes of the New Look. Feet were now a focal point under the new-length swirling, billowing skirts that echoed the Victorian crinolines of the nineteenth century, and Vivier's high-heeled shoes with blunt toes and ankle straps were guaranteed to hold the eye. Dior's designs were the antithesis of the practical wartime look, so too were Vivier's accompanying shoe designs. The immaculate tailoring techniques of the New Look were reflected in shoes that challenged

above *A pair of red satin stilettos by Roger Vivier for Christian Dior (c.1950s) decorated with diamanté-encrusted bows. The streamlining of the shape is echoed in the sleek modernity of the thinner heel.*

right *Tony Armstrong-Jones, later Lord Snowdon, photographed this pair of 1959 Vivier shoes designed for Rayne. Edward Rayne had licensing agreements with many of the leading shoe designers of the day.*

ELLE

Une enquête vitale

sur le problème du logement :

COMMENT
DEVENIR PROPRIÉTAIRE
ET
ÊTRE BIEN CHEZ SOI

UNE HISTOIRE SANS MORALE

par Irwin Shaw

right *Roger Vivier was the first designer used by couturier Christian Dior to have his name featured in its own right. The illustration emphasizes the clean lines of the winklepicker toe.*

by Queen Elizabeth II on her coronation. By 1952 he had created the classic stiletto shoe – a pump shape with a pointed toe and a 10cm (4in) tapered heel. In July of that year US *Vogue* was using the term "stiletto" to describe Vivier's shoes, although many designers such as Charles Jourdan, Herbert Delman, Salvatore Ferragamo, and André Perugia were simultaneously experimenting with tapered heels. With the might of Dior and the respect given to Parisian couture across the world behind him, Vivier was undoubtedly in the right place at the right time.

Vivier's shoes were the height of luxury that could be afforded by few and were not for those who made a habit of walking. As American fashion historian Mary Trasko relates in her book *Heavenly Soles*,

"These gorgeous creations demanded a certain respect ... as a woman found who once purchased a pair of Vivier's rapturously embroidered, very steep stiletto pumps ... She returned the following day with the beadwork slightly torn, complaining that the shoes were uncomfortable. After examining the soles, the manager responded – 'But, Madame, you *walked* in these shoes.'" [xxiii]

This anecdote, although charming, also focuses on one of the fundamental problems in the development of the stiletto – how to keep the heel at once high and durable. Vivier's heel designs of the early 1950s still relied on wood, the traditional material used for heel construction since time immemorial, for the metal backbone of the true stiletto heel had yet to be invented. In fact most early 1950s shoes had comparatively heavy heels, usually a 5cm (2in) thick tapered shape, a more refined type of "Louis" heel that was typical of the popular court shoe. The fantasy stiletto heel was still just that, a fantasy emanating from the drawing boards of fashion designers – it had yet to have any basis in reality. Vivier's heels had to be relatively thick, as the thinner the heel the more likely it was to snap at an inopportune moment. Thus the expectations of the stiletto heel outweighed any technological advance in

Christian Dior

Souliers créés par

Roger Vivier

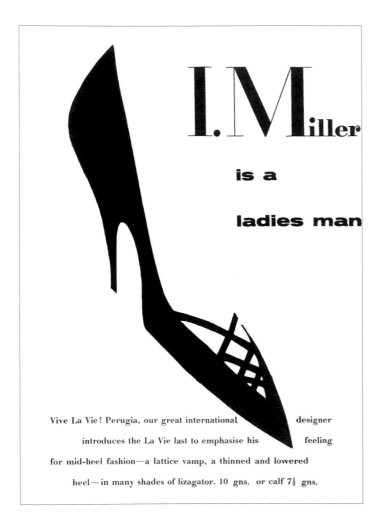

I. Miller

is a

ladies man

Vive La Vie! Perugia, our great international   designer
introduces the La Vie last to emphasise his   feeling
for mid-heel fashion—a lattice vamp, a thinned and lowered
heel—in many shades of lizagator. 10 gns. or calf 7½ gns.

footwear to support it and the elegant modernism of the stiletto as we know it now was not to emanate from Vivier's atelier – nor from that of Italian shoemaker André Perugia, also an early experimenter with the form.

Like Vivier, André Perugia (1893–1977) had a background far removed from the élite world of *haute couture*, although this is where he eventually made his mark designing shoes for Jacques Fath and the House of Schiaparelli on the rue du Faubourg St. Honoré in Paris. During the First World War, Perugia worked in an aeroplane factory, which was to have a profound effect on his design aesthetic, in particular the development of his prototype aerodynamic heels in steel alloy. His 1950 Ode to Industry Shoe was a celebration of the machine age, with a heel of twisted steel that presented a juxtaposition of ergonomics and elegance, as did his 1952 corkscrew heel.

Along with Ferragamo and Vivier, Perugia had begun to make his name in the 1920s and '30s working with such stars as Pola Negri and Gloria Swanson, for whom his black-lace heels became something of a trademark, and the stage star Josephine Baker, for whom he designed a quilted kidskin sandal. In Perugia's eyes shoes spelled sex and he summed up their appeal declaring, "almost every woman is not only conscious of her feet but sex conscious about them." [xxiv] Known for his experimentation with new materials, shapes, and textures Perugia's most successful work was for the American company I. Miller, with whom he had a 50-year association, to be followed by work for Charles Jourdan.

These grandees of *haute couture* were pivotal in the development of the early tapered heel, and were part of a gradual process of experimentation that was going on in shoe design in the early 1950s. They, among others, realized that money was to be made from the 1950s fashion consumer, and an important democratization of fashion emerged with the development of ready-to-wear lines, first by Vivier in 1955 and then in conjunction with Charles Jourdan

for Dior in 1959. Dior's ready-to-wear partnership with Vivier was one of the first instances where a famous master of *haute couture* was prepared to join forces with another designer to explore the potential of a mass-market audience.

It was a venture of incredible success, making Vivier's shoe designs more affordable to a wider market but, at the same time, conveying the magic of the Dior brand. The shoes were enchanted talismans that embodied the chic of the "neatly dressed and coiffed" xxv French *madame* – and represented a purchase of luxury and sophistication for many women. In Britain, hopping across the Channel to the nearest Dior boutique was the embodiment of 1950s glamour and marked one out in relation to one's peers. Barbara Cox, née Godfrey, fondly remembers being transported from the small English coastal town of Deal in Kent to Lille, France, in 1958 to buy her first pair of high-fashion stilettos,

"I went into the Christian Dior boutique and sat down in a grey velvet chair with velvet cushions with 'Christian Dior' written on them in gold. My feet were put on a grey velvet footstool and I was fitted into a pair of soft leather black stilettos ... They fitted really closely to the feet and when you took them off they folded themselves back into a 'Z' shape." xxvi

The connection between luxury shoes and the House of Dior was further consolidated in 1959 when Charles Jourdan designed, manufactured, and distributed shoe models for Dior across the globe. Charles Jourdan (1883–1976) had been an independent shoe manufacturer in the 1920s but after the Second World War his sons René, Charles, and Roland took over the company, launching a woman's boutique in Paris in 1957. Their father was a hard-headed businessman, who realized that the traditional craftsmanship, fit, and quality of *haute couture* shoe design could be successfully transferred to a mass market if the designs were kept simple, yet with a tailored elegance. The actual range of styles should be kept small but shoes could be bought in 20 different colours, three

widths, and many different sizes. A successful brand could then be established with canny advertising campaigns that stressed high fashion at affordable prices. The success of this marketing strategy made the Jourdan name synonymous with shoes that were refined yet accessible and had that couture touch of a perfect "fit." Couture, of course, was all about being fitted, having something that was measured for you, and you alone. As Ginette Spanier, director of the House of Balmain, puts it,

"I have been brought up, like all French-influenced girls, to reverence dress sense, to give clothes emphasis in my thoughts. There is only one way to have your clothes to fit to perfection, and that is to have them fitted. It is logical. That is why women would sooner have a return ticket to Paris, and some francs to spend there, than all the dresses off the pegs of Oxford Street or Fifth Avenue." xxvii

Questioning why women would pay such attention to their clothes, she ponders on whether it is to attract men, or to "knock spots off other women," and concludes,

"Women need the sense of security that the *griffe* gives them. The *griffe* is the little label that the Couture sews into the back of the dress with the great name (Balenciaga, Balmain) on it." xxviii

Fashionable women could enter the portals of a beautifully designed Charles Jourdan boutique, buy a "fitted" shoe with a *griffe* inside, and bask in the associated allure of Parisian chic. Thus women were being encouraged to participate in the new culture of consumption to create an unambiguously Francophile femininity through the use of clothes and cosmetics. As stilettos were the most overtly feminine of objects in the fashion marketplace, they fitted the criteria for wear by a stylish yet still domestic goddess and were also able to signal 1950s modernity over wartime utility. By wearing them, women succeeded in being both the bearers and the creators of beauty, both inside and outside the home, through an awareness

above *The 1961 Agadir stiletto heel by Charles Jourdan with its elegant leather roulade decoration. Jourdan combined quality materials with simple designs to create a mass-market appeal with a* haute couture *brand.*

right *French* haute couture *from the House of Lanvin in 1954 designed by Antonio del Castillo; this displays the severe, sophisticated face of Parisian fashion in the mid-1950s, incorporating high stiletto heels.*

of the latest styles. As design historian Penny Sparke comments, the housewife "could take from the new manifestations of modernism what she wanted and transform or subvert what she did not want." xxix The stiletto was one of the most effective of these manifestations of modernism, both through its commercial success and through the ways in which women used it to say something about themselves in a postwar world.

For a new decade a new vision was necessary and, influenced by the work of Swiss sculptor Alberto Giacometti (1901–66), a love of distorted, attenuated forms became the defining aesthetic of the 1950s – a look that had a profound influence on fashion and shoe design. xxx This new style took its most exaggerated form in the free-standing sculptural Skylon designed by Powell and Moya for the Festival of Britain in 1951, a year-long exhibition aimed at providing a "Tonic to the Nation" after the rigours of wartime rationing. A showcase on the South Bank of London, the Festival publicized Britain to a global market, confidently asserting that regeneration had taken place. The Skylon played with ideas of a thinly tapered shape in the same way that designers began to refine the heel of the fashionable shoe to a gradually sharper and sharper point as the decade progressed. This pencil-thin attenuated line can also be seen in glass and ceramic design and in such iconic pieces as Eero Saarinen's "Tulip chair" designed for Knoll in 1956.

The design historian Thomas Hine also sees in the American stiletto heel a signifier of the new Jet Age that was affecting the look of all aspects of design from Frigidaires to Chevrolets. The jet plane had evolved into a symbol of both physical speed and social transformation, and shoes followed suit. Even though it was an unlikely object to symbolize extremities of motion, associations were made, either through advertising or through the design of the shoes themselves, with the new age of speed. Men's shoes, although conservative in look, were given the veneer of velocity through advertising that juxtaposed the

left *An alternative to the nostalgic New Look crinolined silhouette was this one of sublime streamlining: the attenuated line flowed from the chignon hairstyle through the tight pencil skirt right down to the high stiletto heel.*

classic round-toed brogue with a jet plane or with a Chevy. For women, the *material* design of the shoe embodied the jet age. Hine describes how,

"during the mid-1950s, these went through the same transformation as the jukebox and the Plymouth. In 1954 they were rounded and compact in appearance. In 1956, a shoe of the same size was noticeably longer. The toes were pointed, and in profile the foot rose upward in a more or less continuous line, just like a car with tail-fins … In both cases, practicality was subordinated to the need for a sharp wedge-like profile." xxxi

What could be more attenuated, and thus fashionably experimental and redolent of the new Jet Age, than what UK *Vogue* described in 1950 as "a length of pretty, pretty legs, usually made to seem prettier and more slender because of the high pointed heel" xxxii worn under the ubiquitous pencil skirt. The sheath dress, a 1950s fashion standard, also served as an evocation of this streamlined elegance and, together with heels and seamed stockings, created the length of leg to which women aspired and which was so beloved of couture. The new "clock" stockings with a seam up the back and "fancy designs by the ankle such as swirls and loops" xxxiii made your legs look even longer, and were treasured, as Barbara Cox explains:

"you always bought more than one pair so if one laddered you had another set. In summer we pencilled up the back of our legs with eyebrow pencil to make our legs look longer in our high heels and we tootled along in our tight skirts." xxxiv

Hundreds of beauty books were published counselling women on how to achieve this newly fashionable ideal, and a strict style policy, determined by developments in French *haute couture* with the correct accompanying hairstyle, cosmetics, and shoes, had to be followed if one wanted to appear "well turned out." Women were also supposed to embark on time-consuming beauty routines, for this was the era of advice for the young housewife, mother, and ageing

woman who had to be on her guard at all times to prevent the attentions of her wayward husband from straying. A woman may have lost power in the workforce but through her seduction techniques she could regain power at home. Any kind of beauty activity, even brushing the hair, could be part of an erotic sexual play between a happily married couple, as beauty writer Veronica Dengel explained in enraptured tones,

"You can make a lovely picture in your bedroom if you sit in the soft light and wear a becoming négligé. Brush thoroughly but gracefully, keeping each movement consciously beautiful … when you are fairly proficient, try the effect on your husband. The frequency with which this is injected into pictures about married life proves it is a calculated effect in creating glamour." [xxxv]

Having a good deportment was an identifying mark of the elegant woman and was recognized as such from very early on in the decade. In the immediate postwar years one journalist saw that

"there are not only new clothes but a new way of wearing them; a new way of walking, of standing. The new stance is a hippy one. Your hips become the most prominent part of your body. Your diaphragm above them is taut, so held-in it's practically concave. Your shoulders are held well back. Your seat is tucked away to vanishing point … it's a posture which is very much in tune with the hour." [xxxvi]

This new stance was precisely that played out by Parisian mannequins on the catwalk, and women were tutored how to successfully incorporate Parisian chic into their everyday lives by "learning to be a model at home." [xxxvii] A process of self-surveillance was advised, with information on how to stand and walk the "right way" in the new high heels, with ribs high, shoulders down, and stomach muscles taut. In *How to Keep Pace with Your Daughter* (1958) Ethelind Fearon asked, "Are you properly articulated? Do you swing freely from the hips with knees straight, tummy

and tail tucked in, and chin well up?" [xxxviii] She
recounts the story of a girl who got married on
the strength of her deportment, which was gained
through hours of practice at hip swinging in front
of the mirror at home:

"The result was so perfect that like all the greatest
works of art and craft, it looked natural and
spontaneous. It also looked like Garbo and a cheetah,
and all her young men raved about her 'lovely lope'
even though it was the only thing she had. You might
think that to put one foot before the other and repeat
ad lib or da capo was a natural and universal
accomplishment, but … it takes practice." [xxxix]

The new, tapered high heels were part of this look and
beauty books gave advice on deportment and posture,
emphasizing heels as formal rather than everyday
wear. As Betty Page advised in her book *On Fair
Vanity* (1954), "Shoes with heels of the right height,
so that you can walk with grace and ease, are in far
better taste than the smartest shoes with 4in [10cm]
heels in which you waddle like a duck." [xl] And Eileen
McCarthy in *Frankly Feminine* (1965) wrote,

"Heel heights should be right for you and right for
the clothes you're wearing. Moderate heels are best.
A short woman in spike heels is as obviously
compensation-conscious as a tall woman in flat-heeled
shoes. When her heels are too high a short-legged
woman tends to walk stiffly and rivet attention on the
lack of length in her leg from knee to heel." [xli]

It began to be acknowledged, then, that the stiletto
heel could cause problems. In 1953, *Picture Post* was
one of the first publications to publicize the new
stiletto heel, "which has just reached London, at last,
from Paris," [xlii] yet at the same time warned of its
disadvantages. In a feature entitled "The Hazards of
the Stiletto Heel," an English model was required to
try out a pair around London. Accordingly she was
documented falling over, getting her heel caught in
pavement gratings, and generally seeming rather
foolish. The magazine also noted that,

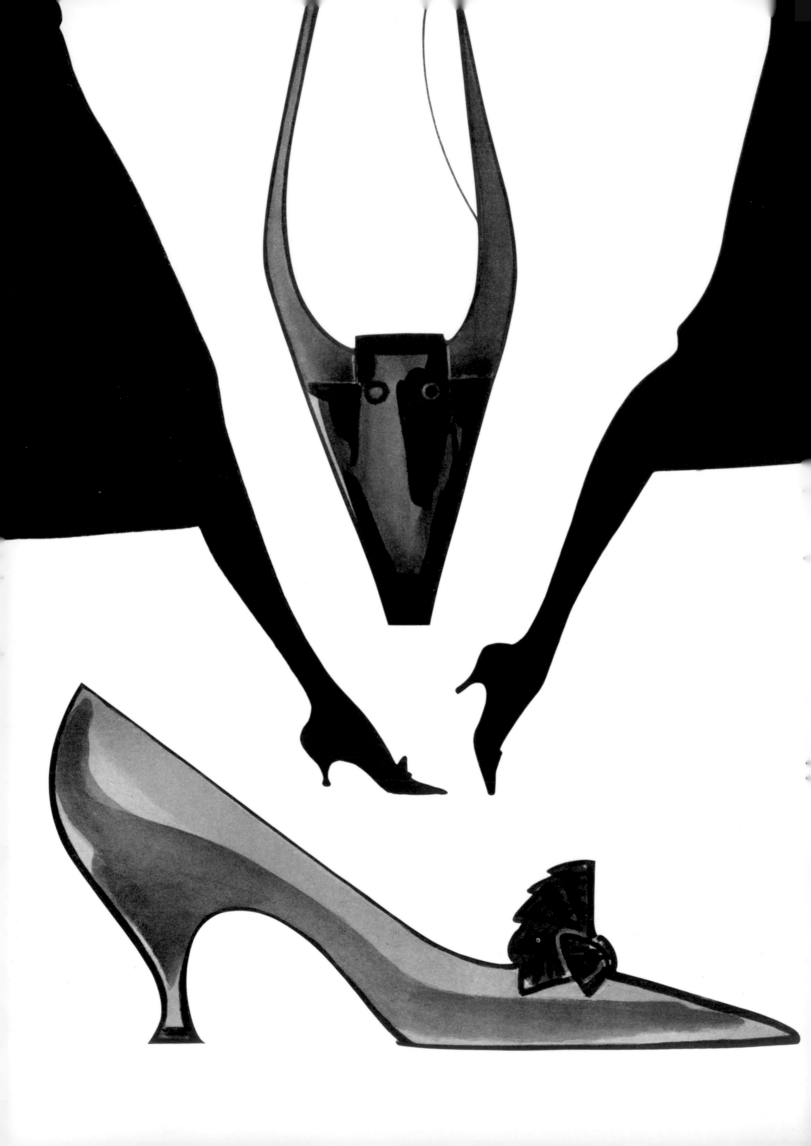

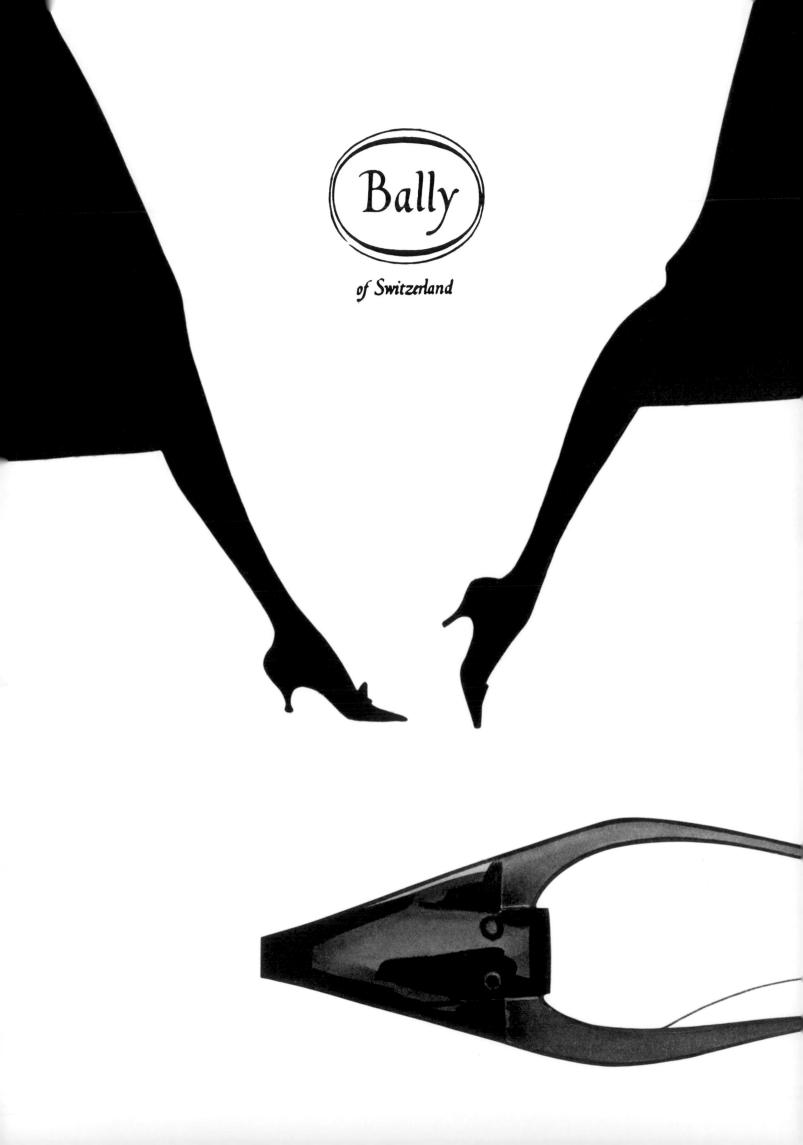

"Doctors are already protesting that the 10cm (4in) heel, with a tiny base … will harm a girl's feet. Dressmakers welcome it, as it compels the wearer to take tiny steps … it cannot do much harm, if only worn occasionally. In any case girls will wear it." xliii

This early warning showed the conflicting perspectives over the stiletto heel: it may have been uncomfortable and difficult to walk around in, but women wanted it nevertheless.

One of the first manufacturers to accede to the demand for the British stiletto heel was Gina, formerly Mexico Shoes, who set up in the East End of London in 1954. After making cork platforms and wedges in the early 1950s, founder, owner, and father of the current owners, Mehmet Kurdash, was approached by a retailer who was being overwhelmed by the demand for the stiletto from British women. Using reject heels from Hollis, a carpentry firm that, like Gina, recognized the potential of this new shoe and had moved into heel production, Kurdash began designing and producing some of the most glamorous shoes in Europe using one of the earliest stiletto heels. To achieve the thinnest heel, Kurdash used Hollis wood heels with an aluminium spigot that reached from the steel tip to the body of the shoe, and then encased the whole heel in leather. These early British stilettos were immediately successful and the company has never stopped production, progressing from an initial 70 pairs per week to between 800 and 1000 by the new millennium. As Kurdash explains, "We never stopped making stilettos. Ladies like them, they make their bodies swing. Every generation needs to try them out." xliv

As the decade progressed, more murmurings were heard about the new, increasingly tapered stiletto heel. Many women were ambivalent about wearing them and not everyone approved. A Miss M. Marshall of Bexhill, England, wrote to a popular daily newspaper in 1957,

"Men are attracted by high heels. I know that when I wear a pair of 5in [12cm] stiletto heels a man is

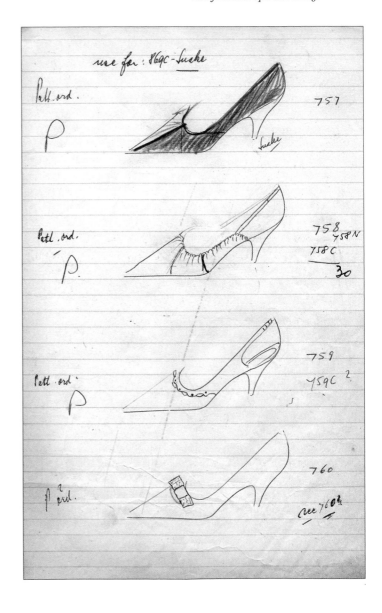

not only attracted, he is fascinated. Can you wonder that smart women wear the highest, slenderest heels they can obtain?" xlv

However, someone signing herself "Professional of Kent" argued more prosaically,

"I wonder if those men who proclaim their admiration for women in high heels would be prepared to subject themselves to such torture, and furthermore risk the danger of injuring themselves for life? If girls (and the men, too) could walk through one of our foot hospitals when operating was in progress, they would soon form a different opinion of incorrect footwear." xlvi

It is here, then, that we begin to see the lines of the great stiletto debate being drawn, which was to dominate its next incarnation in the late 1950s. Did the stiletto somehow symbolize the subjugation of women in the 1950s or was it a sign of open resistance by women? Its use as a rite of passage, a passing from girlhood to the full sexual maturity of a woman, could represent an emergence into a world of feminine power, albeit a conservative one based around fashionable consumption. From the flat-heeled, broad-toed shoe of the child, through the kitten heel of the teenager to the full blown 10cm (4in) stiletto there seems to be a very powerful if paradoxical invocation of femininity at work. For instance, how could you do housework in circle skirts and spindly heels? But at the same time needle heels were uncomfortable, physically restricting, and bad for the feet. Perhaps this new look could be read as less an embracing of woman's domestic role as a rejection of it, a sign of open resistance, a challenge to male-dominated culture by wearing shoes that quite clearly signalled, "I haven't tidied up today." Or was it merely a trivial fashion worn by foolish women who should know better? A moral panic was about to ensue as a result of the next incarnation of the stiletto – less French chic, more wild style – and the site of the next set of key developments was no longer Paris but Italy.

Un joli bas, c'est autre chose...

portez le bas

Scandale

HOLLYWOOD HEELS

"You are flirting with danger

when you buy high-heeled sandals."

Eileen Allen, The Book of Beauty (1961)

high treason!

Airborne PARIS POINTS *were designed by an Italian!*

With reason...the austerité, sévérité, simplicité of the Gallic school is warmed, softened, sleeked and speeded with Roman bravura to shape the lithest, loveliest shoes of the century... Airborne's Paris Points.

previous page *Marilyn Monroe's red rhinestone stiletto heel was designed by Salvatore Ferragamo in the early 1950s and sold at Christie's, London, in 1999 for £23,500 ($42,000). The shoes are now housed in the Salvatore Ferragamo Museum in Florence.*

left *This 1960 advertisement for Paris Points shows how the dominance of the French stiletto was being challenged by the Italian shoe, which was altogether higher, sharper, and sexier.*

I n Italy the story of the stiletto is altogether different, and represents something of a divergence from the high art of Roger Vivier in the ateliers of Paris where the needle heels that we associate with the term "stiletto" today were created. In Italy, the period of 1945 to 1965 (now known as the Ricostruzione) was one of unparalleled economic and cultural change, a time of social and material revolution after years of Fascism. Following the Second World War, Italy underwent reconstruction abetted by massive economic aid from the United States which, in an attempt to boost postwar trade, was helping to regenerate large areas of the Continent. This was thus a favourable time for Italian industry and helped to strengthen Italian fashion as a brand in which shoes had always played an important part. Italian shoemakers, like French hairdressers, enjoyed an enviable reputation for their craftsmanship which had endured for decades and had spawned such global stars as Salvatore Ferragamo, "the Shoemaker of Dreams." [ii]

After his apprenticeship in Italy, Bonito-born Ferragamo (1898–1960) migrated to Santa Barbara, California, in 1914, where he set up an exclusive business specializing in handmade shoes and repairs. His hand-wrought designs, which like those of Vivier combined exquisitely ornamental forms with function, were discovered by the American Film Corporation in 1914. The heroes of their popular Western sagas were shod in Ferragamo boots so comfortable that the director Cecil B. De Mille was heard to comment, "The West would have been conquered earlier if they had had boots like these." [iii] Ferragamo's fame spread fast among the movie crowd based in Santa Barbara and his business became a "shoe-shop to the stars," [iv] including such clients as Mary Pickford, Pola Negri, Clara Bow, and Rudolph Valentino. Gloria Swanson inspired some of his most extravagant fantasies – it was for her that he created his famed corkscrew heels bedecked with real pearls. The Ferragamo heel was typically made of wood covered in a luscious material such as gold kid or satin, and there was also his inventive hollow "cage" heel of filigree brass.

Soon the demand for Ferragamo shoes was such that
it caused real problems for his business. Unwilling to
sacrifice quality for quantity, and realizing that the
skills of the American shoe worker could not cope
with the demands of production on a larger scale,
Ferragamo moved back to Italy in 1927, settling in
Florence. The city was home to dozens of small firms
specializing in luxury leather goods and possessing
the high level of expertise that had been missing in
California. Here he established what was to become
one of the most famous shoe companies of the
twentieth century, making the name of Ferragamo
synonymous with Florence and innovative shoe
design. Italian shoemakers no longer produced
imitations of French couture styles, but were defining
an aesthetic that was all their own. Using American
techniques of mass production together with the
craftsmanship of Italian luxury goods, Ferragamo
created cutting-edge footwear for the international
jet set, in turn establishing his own international
reputation. This fame, and concomitantly that of
the Italian shoe industry, was further consolidated
in 1947 when he was presented with the prestigious
American Neiman Marcus award, the fashion
equivalent of an Oscar. As Ferragamo later stressed,

"Women must be persuaded that luxury shoes
need not be painful to walk in; they must be
convinced that it is possible to wear the most
refined and exotic footwear because we know
how to design a supportive shoe modelled to the
shape of the foot. Elegance and comfort are not
incompatible, and whoever maintains the contrary
simply doesn't know what he is talking about." [v]

The consolidation of Italy as an international centre
of fashion innovation continued with the help of
the Italian government. Ferragamo became an
ambassador of Italian style working for the officially
sanctioned "Made in Italy" promotion. This global
campaign was set up to heavily promote the Italian
look and made household names of fashion designer
Emilio Pucci (1914–92) and product designer Gio
Ponti (1891–1979), as well as positioning Florence as

DAKS REGD

Simpson TAILORED

365 YMY.

a fashion centre and general home to good taste. As a re-branding exercise to help the country redefine itself as a centre of design innovation in the global marketplace after the Second World War it couldn't have been more successful, and a process of dissociation began. Italy changed from a country indicative of Mussolini's Fascist project to a land of glamorous *dolce vita* – the words "Italian design" were beginning to become synonymous with stylish living.

Italy continued steadily building on an enviable reputation for shoe design and exquisite craftsmanship, and by the mid-1950s designers were taking Vivier's tapered heel shape and exaggerating it to even more extreme proportions. Manufacturers sought the solution to the ultimate problem – how to create a viable yet commercial stiletto heel that fulfilled the fantasy of its name and the dreams of fashion designers still searching for the perfectly attenuated shape. Lee Wright in his essay "Objectifying Gender: The Stiletto Heel" describes how a strong heel could be gained by using interlocking pieces of wood, but,

"Paradoxically, the heel which had consumer credibility in terms of wear was too heavy and clumsy to warrant the title of stiletto, while the one which did warrant the title by successfully reproducing the fashionable form did not stand up to wear. Pressure to produce the stiletto at this point seems to have come from the fashion industry, which continued to promote this airy, streamlined shoe." vi

By 1955 manufacturers in Italy were realizing that a slim wooden heel would never be strong enough to withstand the wear and tear of life in a modern city so other materials began to enter into the equation. Mehmet Kurdash, founder of Gina, had been using an aluminium spigot in Britain as early as 1954 and by 1956 another solution was exhibited at an Italian trade fair. It was here that the slenderness of the spiked shoe together with its teetering height could be seen, this construction made possible by a metal spigot being enclosed in a plastic heel shell which prevented breakage. With this design, heels could be ultra thin but perfectly reliable, less prone to

above *A series of high spike-heel designs by Salvatore Ferragamo from 1956. Ferragamo's stilettos were worn by the sexiest Hollywood stars. This helped shift the perception of the stiletto from French chic towards Italian sensuality.*

left *A Daks advert of 1961 using the vogue for Italian styling to sell British products. The model poses on a scooter and wears white stilettos, the height of shoe fashion in the early 1960s.*

opposite *By the early 1960s the most extreme of heels was now technically possible and no longer the fantasy of fashion illustrators. The kitten heel (the white shoe opposite) was worn by many teenagers as a "training" shoe.*

below *In 1960 the winklepicker shoe with stiletto heel and an extreme point to the toe was heralded as a new teenage fashion. It quickly became a symbol of teenage rebellion, as easily decoded as the black leather jacket.*

snapping and breaking – a 12cm (5in) heel became almost standard by the end of the 1950s.

The toes of the stiletto shoe were later elongated into long points reminiscent of the "poulaine," a shoe shape in vogue from the twelfth to the fifteenth centuries in Europe. These long, tapering shoes worn by men were an impractical, dandified fashion "which had much the same effect as the codpiece a couple of centuries later: it glorified masculine sexuality in a most obvious way." [vii] This became a new shape for women in the early 1960s, dubbed "winklepickers," and when complemented with high pin-sharp heels tapered to rapier-like points, one of the longest-running and ultimately successful shoes of the twentieth and twenty-first centuries was created.

Italy now became the established centre of directional shoe design and from the mid-1950s onward fashionable footwear was always assumed to have a "Made in Italy" label. Even Gina shoes, a success in their own right, used Italian references to associate its shoes with the quality footwear of Italy. Gina was named after the popular Italian film star Gina Lollobrigida, as founder Kurdash explains: "it was a short name, easy to pronounce and she was very fashionable." [viii] Inside every Gina shoe was the legend "Ispirazione Italiana," despite their being an entirely British design and production. Vivier responded with the *talon aiguille* or "needle heel" in 1955 which was finely tapered and reinforced with steel but, in that very same year, Albanese and Dal Co, both shoe manufacturers based in Rome, were climbing to even higher heights with their more affordable "killer heels." Ferragamo's most vertiginous heel designs arrived a little later, between 1958 and 1959. Shoe designers in other countries began to follow suit, among them Bally of Switzerland, Russell & Bromley in England, and Delman and Saks on Fifth Avenue in New York.

Italy was seen as the place to be in the mid-1950s, and provided a rich fantasy of Continental life that was in turn sold to a global audience through Hollywood

films such as *Roman Holiday* (1953) and *Three Coins in a Fountain* (1954). The Italian film industry based at Cinecittà in Rome also played its part in concocting a heady mix of sun, sea, and film stars, juxtaposing Sophia Loren, Portofino, and Ferragamo heels to invent a new kind of Italian glamour. Living *la dolce vita* were stars as diverse as Gina Lollobrigida and Anna Magnani; the latter, although known for the earthy realism of her roles, wore Ferragamos when appearing in public.

Italy was also responsible for a change in the notion of what constituted good taste in popular style. On the one hand there was the rationalist design for industry, and on the other what design consultant Stephen Bayley describes as "a popular visual culture that produced such evocative symbols as the Vespa, the sharply tailored mohair suit, and the hissing Gaggia coffee machines …" ix Taste was no longer the province of the educated élite but was predicated on the demands of a more populist consumer culture which demanded design that was modern, deluxe, fashionable, and, above all else, glamorous. This feeling was exacerbated by the death of Christian Dior in 1957. The hold that *haute couture* had had over the changing styles and silhouettes of 1950s fashion was loosening, mass styles were beginning to emanate from the sidewalk rather than the catwalk – and a freer form of cross-fertilization was taking place.

Italian style was an important foundation for an emerging teenage culture, particularly in Britain – a look that was perceived to be one of style and sophistication by its teenage aficionados, who first discovered it at the local picture house. For Barbara Cox, going to the movies three times a week formed the main part of her leisure activity, "the biggest event of our lives," x where she watched both Anglo-American and subtitled European films at the Royal cinema in Deal, Kent. Sophia Loren, Marina Vladi, Rossano Brazzi, and Gina Lollobrigida were her favourite stars and she, like many other young women in the late 1950s and early '60s, copied their style avidly. For Barbara, "Gina Lollobrigida was in the

right *Fellini's* La Dolce Vita *gripped audiences across the world in 1960, depicting a lifestyle that seemed to speak of unbridled sexuality and a passion for Italian fashion – in which the stiletto played a significant part.*

forefront with tight elastic belts, loads of frou-frou skirts underneath, short white gloves, and very high stilettos," and she created her own version of this Italian starlet look involving glazed cotton dresses with bright flowers and dirndl skirts, hooped earrings, and lashings of lipstick. Her husband remembers hanging out in "Devito's milk bar, acting out *La Dolce Vita* with frothy coffee." [xi]

By 1962 the Italian look had gripped London in a veritable revolution in British popular taste. It found expression in the cult of the Italian motor scooter – Lambrettas and Vespas, espresso coffee machines, and the stiletto – what the writer Toni del Renzio in 1957 dubbed "a genuine urban folk art." [xii] For teenagers, Continental design seemed to embody the chic modernity of everything that was lacking in stodgy postwar Britain and this was a time in their lives when they had money and leisure time with which to indulge. Four million kids between the ages of 13 and 25 had economic strength and, with their estimated spending power of 900 million pounds, could seriously affect the teenage market. Len Deighton expresses this obsession with buying into European culture in *The Ipcress File* when describing his hero walking through London,

"… down Charlotte Street towards Soho. It was that sort of January morning that has enough sunshine to point up the dirt without raising the temperature. I was probably seeking excuses to delay; I bought two packets of Gauloises, sank a quick grappa with Mario and Franco at the Terazza, bought a *Statesman*, some Normandy butter, and garlic sausage." [xiii]

Continental style was part of a general aesthetic of "cool" that had invaded youth culture, raising an awareness of European modes of behaviour and introducing youth culture to the elegance and sharpness of Italian design. Emilio Pucci, Fontana, and Gio Ponti were magical names appearing in all the right style magazines and were enthusiastically embraced by teenagers. They appealed particularly to Mods, who arrived on the Soho scene in the late

Vietato ai minori di 16 anni
DISTRIBUZIONE
CINERIZ
FEDERICO FELLINI
LA
DOLCE
VITA
TOTALSCOPE
MARCHIO DEPOSITATO DALL'A.T.C.
MARCELLO MASTROIANNI
ANITA EKBERG
ANOUK AIMEE · YVONNE FURNEAUX · ALAIN CUNY · ANNIBALE NINCHI
e MAGALI NOEL · LEX BARKER · JACQUES SERNAS e con NADIA GRAY
WALTER SANTESSO · UNA CO-PRODUZIONE RIAMA FILM, ROMA - PATHE CONSORTIUM CINEMA, PARIGI
REALIZZATA DA GIUSEPPE AMATO

left *A young woman in the early 1960s wearing the Italian look: dirndl skirts in bright prints worn with sugar-starched petticoats and high spiked heels.*

1950s displaying in their elegance a fascination with Italian tailoring and a general Continental aesthetic. In his seminal novel *Absolute Beginners* (1959), writer Colin MacInnes describes this burgeoning teenage culture, initially centred around London's Soho in the late 1950s. Italian-style references feature heavily throughout the book, functioning as a clear declaration of independence from the unfashionable adult world of postwar Britain. The absolute beginners, the book's eponymous heroes, concoct their own urban argot of cool music and casually elegant "teenage drag." [xiv] Seemingly infused with the steam of a Gaggia coffee machine, the novel introduces such characters as Suzette, whom we meet in a "Belgravia coffee bar ... called the Last Days of Pompeii," where "she was allowing her capuccino to grow cold. She looked dreamy, and actually flipped her eyelashes in the Italian starlet manner." [xv]

Soho Mods were relatively affluent and obsessive almost fetishistic – about the cut of their clothes. Subverting the British country style of tailored suits in mohair or houndstooth check, male Mods prided themselves on their tailored elegance, and boutiques sprang up to cater for them on Carnaby Street. John Stephen shirts, Nero haircuts, and popped purple hearts (amphetamines) were the order of the day for a lifestyle that revolved around the hedonism of consumption. Girls wore the most up-to-date fashions – all beehive hairstyles and Italian stilettos. MacInnes summarily details the look of the Dean, the perfect Mod:

"College-boy smooth crop hair with burned-in parting, neat white Italian round-collared shirt, short Roman jacket very tailored (two little vents, three buttons) no turn-up narrow trousers with 17in [43cm] bottoms absolute maximum, pointed-toe shoes, and a white mac folded by his side." [xvi]

Significantly his girlfriend, "a Modern jazz boy's girl," sported "... short hemlines, seamless stockings, pointed-toe high-heeled stiletto shoes, crepe nylon rattling petticoat, short blazer jacket, hair done up into the elfin style." [xvii]

This Italian starlet look was also given a boost by Hollywood. In the United States the stiletto heel had been imported from Italy and was being worn by the sexiest of stars by the late 1950s. "I don't know who invented high heels but all women owe him a lot," murmured Marilyn Monroe [xviii], whose Ferragamo heels with metal reinforcements were a significant trademark. Known from very early on in her career for a particularly sexy style of walking, she was asked to test for a Marx Brothers movie *Love Happy* in 1949. Hollywood writer Maurice Zolotow described how Groucho and Harpo "examined her, looking at her, she says, 'like I was a piece of French pastry.'" Monroe didn't have any lines to speak; the idea was that she would do the talking with her body:

"'Can you walk?' Groucho asked. She assured him she had never had any complaints. 'But,' questioned Groucho, 'can you walk so you'll make smoke come out of my head?' She walked. Just across the room, but it was enough. 'She walks like a rabbit,' said Groucho approvingly, as he brushed wisps of smoke away from his head." [xix]

Throughout her career, speculation was rife over what made Marilyn walk in that particular way. Explanations included a swimming accident, double-jointed knees, and a fractured ankle as a child – all of which she denied, saying,

"I've never done anything deliberately about the way I walk. People say I walk all wiggly and wobbly, but I don't know what they mean. I just walk. I've never wriggled deliberately in my life, but all my life I've had trouble with people who say I do." [xx]

Was she being disingenuous? Jimmy Starr, former columnist on the *Los Angeles Herald Express*, claimed to know the secret: "She learned a trick of cutting a quarter of an inch off one heel so that when she walked, that little fanny would wriggle." [xxi] This would have been an expensive business, for Marilyn was renowned for her love of Ferragamo stilettos. She was the proud owner of 40 pairs, ranging from

right *The sweater-girl look was pure pneumatic 1950s: here, the model's tight top reveals a circular stitched Triumph Whirlpool bra, while a pair of the highest, thinnest heels adorns her feet.*

the scarlet satin pair encrusted with scarlet rhinestones (see p.54) worn in the show-stopping number "Two Little Girls from Little Rock" sung with Jane Russell in *Gentlemen Prefer Blondes* (1953) to black satin and gold kidskin for everyday wear. She had tips for her female audience too:"Always wear flesh-coloured shoes with flesh-coloured tights, black with black and always, always high heels, because it lengthens the leg." xxii Following her own mantra, she commissioned unique flesh-toned silk stiletto heels from Ferragamo, remarking archly that his shoes had "given a lift" to her career. xxiii

With her spike-heeled stilettos and tight pencil skirts or hip-hugging Capri pants, Marilyn gave a global audience of cinema-goers a reincarnation of the "sweater girl" look that had been a firm favourite in cheesecake glamour imagery since the 1940s – all sexy suggestiveness and mass-market glamour. In her novel of 1960, *The L-Shaped Room*, Lynne Reid Banks makes fun of a budding starlet who appears at a press call sporting this typical style:

"The red hair flowed over bare white shoulders. The celebrated bust, looking like two dunce's caps applied to her chest, was encased in a puce halter-neck sweater which left all but the essentials bare. Her sizeable bottom and not-too-marvellous legs were thinly coated with bright-yellow silk jeans ending just below the knee; her bare feet were thrust into pink mules with diamond spike-heels." xxiv

The sweater-girl look was copied by many women for whom cinema provided a form of escape – a release from their domestic duties. Like the stiletto itself, the sweater-girl image began to be read as anti-maternal, a notion alluded to as early as 1954 in this verse by beauty writer Betty Page,

"Look out, you Sweater Girls!
Sooner or later
The mode will change to
Something straighter
Reverting to the mode of mater." xxv

Week ending November 27 1958
EVERY THURSDAY 19

Picturegoer

THE NATIONAL FILM WEEKLY

LL OPEN YOUR EYES
ON HOLLYWOOD

BY

RITA GAM

Working with
Shelley Winters

by

JOHN GREGSON

CLEO MOORE
One hundred and eleven
sweaters help her aim
to "keep dressed up"
— see page 23

Women analysed the fashions shown on the screen in detail, relishing the luxury of the *mise-en-scène* and the lavish interior of the cinema building itself. Hollywood offered a vision of an enticing world and its glamorous stars were a key source of pleasure. The high heel had long been a fashion fixture on the screen, part of cinematic vocabulary, appearing variously on the foot of the *femme fatale* of the 1940s film *noir* and the sexy sweater girl of the 1950s. In fact the tracking shot from the heel of the shoe to the top of the thigh had become something of a cliché, signalling a sexually desirable, almost wanton vamp. Similarly, a passionate kiss followed by a close-up of a stiletto heel gently falling off a foot, then a fade-out, meant a very passionate interlude was taking place. And what more compelling combination of star and stiletto could there be than Frank Sinatra quaffing champagne from a shoe in *High Society* (1950) or Anita Ekberg in *La Dolce Vita* (1960) cavorting in a fountain and drinking champagne from a stiletto? A new cinematic ideal of glamour and rebellion (and it could be said somewhat of an oral-genital fantasy) was being created through the use of the stiletto.

By the late 1950s the stiletto was being worn by stars who had a reputation for being rather risqué – charismatic, rather knowing women famed as much for their tempestuous affairs in real life as on screen. Marilyn Monroe, Ava Gardner, Jayne Mansfield, and the British Diana Dors transgressed the codes of respectable domestic femininity. By holding themselves up for inspection on the silver screen they made it plain to the viewer the lack of glamour to be found in motherhood. Thus for many women the American star in stilettos displayed a new identity far removed from that of their mothers – one that was exciting, colourful, almost brash. Through consuming commodities that seemed on a par with those of their chosen Hollywood star, women could bring their object of desire closer to themselves and mark themselves out from the older generation. As Ken Cox, a teenager in the 1950s, remarked, "stiletto heels made girls' ankles look different to my mother's," [xxvi] and in Stan Barstow's

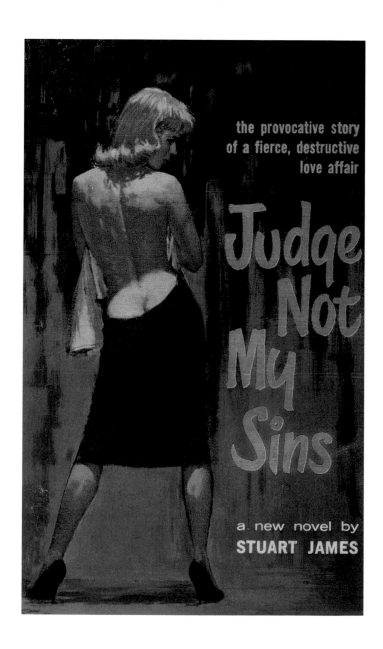

the provocative story of a fierce, destructive love affair

Judge Not My Sins

a new novel by
STUART JAMES

opposite *Mamie van Doren in* High School Confidential *in 1959 shows how the stiletto was no longer the mark of the chic Parisienne, but symbolized a more earthbound yet glamorous Hollywood sexuality.*

below *Sweater-girl incarnate Jayne Mansfield, whose breasts were reputedly insured for one million dollars poses in her stiletto mules with white mink coat outside Elstree Studios in 1959.*

1960 novel *A Kind of Loving* a sharp differentiation is made between the rather dull good girls, who wore flats, and the high heels of the local sweater girls, working-class sex bombs. The protagonist describes going to the Gala Rooms where he is almost knocked over by a couple dancing,

"The bint he's doing his stuff with is a real case, all eyebrows and lipstick with a white complexion that makes her look like death warmed up, and two under the front of her black sweater that stick out like chapel hat-pegs, brassiered till it must be agony, and nearly taking this bloke's eye out the way he's half doubled up breathing all over her chest." xxvii

Stilettos spelled sex, and aping the Monroe wiggle was a prerequisite of sporting the shoe. The high heel forced the wearer to tilt forward and by doing so caused her bottom and breasts to thrust outward, thus highlighting the sexual zones of her body. Pushing the body forward in such a way also caused that particular undulation that many men responded to because of its very blatant sexuality. For one newly married man in *A Kind of Loving*, the gait of the stiletto-shod girl symbolized his own loss of freedom,

"As we go through the gates into the street a bint goes by, wobbling a bit on stiletto heels. I sort of half-register the fact that she's got nice legs and then all at once it comes over me that I'll never be able to look at a bint with an open mind again. I'm a goner. The search is over for me. I'm a married man as of five minutes ago." xxviii

The late-1950s stiletto in its aggressively modern form rejected humble domesticity. The obvious impracticality of the shoe was a clear sign of open resistance by women who were challenging their predetermined domestic roles. What was once considered to be a decorative evening shoe was appropriated by young women and worn as an overtly sexual shoe for everyday wear, displaying an open rebellion through sartorial chic. Some men found this display of Hollywood glamour rather

KAYSER
BONDOR

incongruous in an everyday setting. In his 1957 novel *A Room at the Top*, John Braine describes a young woman with

"a round flat face with lipstick the wrong shade. Her silk stockings and high heels struck an incongruously voluptuous note, it was as if she were scrubbing floors in a transparent nylon nightie." xxix

The new durable plastic heels made the widespread wearing of the stiletto possible and, from 1957, true stilettos using the new Italian techniques of a metal spigot encased in plastic had begun to be readily available outside of Italy. In Britain, for instance, that same year a heel-component company imported the technology after buying up the rights from the original Italian manufacturers. Mehmet Kurdash of Gina shoes remembered buying "injection-moulded plastic heels with a steel tube inside like a long nail. The heel came in long lengths that could be cut off at any point you liked." xxx Injection-moulding techniques used for the heels meant the stiletto could be produced quickly, cheaply, and in large numbers – something that many women were demanding. Glamour girl Jayne Mansfield had a reputed 200 pairs of stiletto heels and girls wanted to catch up!

The mastery of the 12cm (5in) stiletto heel became a badge of audacious femininity. By the end of the 1950s the stiletto encompassed everything that was right about modern style. It was sleek, sharp, and sexy with an aura of elegant menace, and as slender, tapered, and dangerous as the eponymous Sicilian fighting knife it was named after. The Italian stiletto knife, an elegant and swift "shiv," was a 14cm (5½in) switchblade associated in the popular consciousness with the wild motorbike hoodlums of *The Wild One* (1954), starring the moody Marlon Brando, and the Puerto Rican street gangs of *West Side Story* (1958). In the form of the flick knife the stiletto conjured up the juvenile delinquency of the Teddy Boys, whose Edwardian suits could conceal razors, coshes, and stealthy cutters. The stiletto shoe itself could be used as an effective weapon by women, one wearer remembering a sharpened heel

left Shirley MacLaine played French prostitute Irma in Dance in the 1963 film of the same name. The dress codes of the streetwalker in this period included a split skirt and stiletto heels.

being ground gently "into a guy's foot if he got too fresh." Men at the time treated stiletto wearers with respect, for "when you were dancing and one went on your foot, ten stone down to less than half an inch square, the actual pressure was one hundred pounds per square inch." It could be used even more violently when taken off. In the cult book *Generation X* of 1964 one young prostitute says vehemently of her pimp, "There were times when I could have murdered Johnny. I've been so mad ... that I've gone for him with anything I could lay my hands on - a knife, a stiletto shoe, anything ..."

As an object of consumption, the stiletto embodied the pleasures and dangers of the city street and had become a pivotal part of a new fashion vocabulary for girls who walked on the wild side. In Lynne Reid Banks' 1960 novel *The L-Shaped Room*, a young prostitute gropes "under the bed for her shoes. They were light beige, with high heels. They're Italian ... ever so smart. Soft, too. I spend a lot on shoes. It's worth it when you're on your feet so much." The higher the stiletto, the more wild the girl. Barbara Cox, a young woman at the time, explained, "Real totterers, over four foot high were worn by 'fast' girls," and recalled one 1950s teenager joking, "they were the ones the boys went for." Stilettos were "knock-'em-dead weapons as well as footwear. Hard to walk in, but so sophisticated. We just had to remember to stay away from gratings and escalators." The writer Angela Carter described her own personal challenge to the style conventions of late 1950s femininity: "When I was 18 I went rigged out in all the atrocious sartorial splendour of the underground high style of the late 1950s; black mesh stockings, spike-heeled shoes, bum-hugging skirt, jacket with a black fox collar." But there were many others.

"At one time I had a black beehive three feet high like a Guardsman's bearskin, which I wore with white winklepickers and black stockings ... I jived like a demon to Little Richard ... then I made my way home ... My parents must not wake to find it was half past four ..."

And you could hear the bad girls advancing: "I got my first pair of real heels in the eighth grade. They had metal tips and you could hear me coming three blocks away." xxxviii By 1959 the stiletto had reached its most extreme height, 15cm (6in) of sharpened steel with a plastic coating, its tiny heel refined to needle thin, the iron tip causing sparks to fly but also sparking howls of protest. As the stiletto grew more pointed and blatantly sexual, its meaning became more frank and thus harder to ignore. A moral panic broke out in the popular media very similar in essence to the outrage caused by the bobbed haircut for women in the 1920s. Newly bobbed women had been openly asserting their independence through a fashionable look and the concomitant "problem" of the Amazonian woman of the 1920s became a popular subject for discussion. Similarly with the stiletto, when associations began to be made in the popular consciousness with a more independent form of female sexuality – perhaps even the creation of a new race of sexually predatory women – a moral furore ensued.

The result was that the problems of both the bob in the 1920s and the stiletto in the late 1950s and early '60s were medicalized. Women shorn of their hair were warned that they risked it growing back somewhere else, particularly on the chin, and that cutting their hair would sap their strength. In much the same way, stiletto wearers were warned that they risked deforming their feet as a result of the toe-crippling fit combined with the height of the heels. Attacks on the stiletto, the majority made by men in the medical profession, were rife. As early as 1952, Dr George Bankoff in his beauty primer for women, *The Essential Eve: A Guide to Woman's Perfection*, gave vent to his scorn for the high-heeled shoe, saying:

"Excessively high heels will always be a source of danger to feet and eventually to health. Their habitual use causes the calf muscles to contract to such an extent that ... it becomes almost impossible to walk either barefoot or in slippers ... Thick ankles and mildly deformed feet are among the direct products of shoes with 6in [15cm] heels." xxxix

right *Elizabeth Taylor in* Cat on a Hot Tin Roof *(1958) in an outfit befitting her role as a sex siren: tight pencil skirt, stockings, and a pair of vertiginous heels.*

Two teenage girls in London in 1960 wearing the most extreme forms of winklepicker stilettos. To this age group, they seemed to represent an active rebellion against the notion that women should remain in the domestic sphere looking after hearth and home.

And in 1960 another expert, Harry Roberts, in his book *The Practical Way to Keep Fit*, rejected the new shoe stating that, "the faults of the conventional female shoe of the period are almost infinite in number, and utterly gross and fundamental in character." [xl] He goes on to state that the stiletto has none of the useful purposes of a shoe, and is simply an invitation to "potential evil."

"Its absurd general shape ... its ridiculous narrowness and exaggerated heels, all are calculated not only to throw all parts of one of our most delicate and important structures out of position, but also to cramp and pinch into a shapeless heap the hundreds of sensitive muscles, ligaments, nerves ... The modern shoe, with its torturings and hamperings, has done much to send walking out of fashion." [xli]

One male foot specialist decried "juvenile shoe delinquency," saying that "teenagers, too, are becoming addicts of court shoes, pencil-heeled with toes as sharp as the fangs of the biblical serpent." [xlii] The headmaster of a secondary school in Surrey, England, also expressed his fear of youth out of control: "High heels can cause the downward path. High heels and winklepickers can lead to delinquency if worn at school." [xliii] In Mobile, Alabama, the authorities were taking no chances. Shoes with heels more than 2.5cm (1in) high and less than 2.5cm (1in) thick were declared illegal. The chief of police stated, "no arrests are expected, but the City will not be responsible for accidents in the streets, when women fall over gratings, cement joints, etc., causing broken arms, skinned noses, twisted legs, and loss of dignity." [xliv]

British teenagers were advised a little more gently in *Modern Living: Your Looks* (1963) to avoid the stiletto shoe at all costs. Warning of its deforming effects but also of the demands on the wearer's dignity, author Mary Davis Peters counselled the teenage consumer to avoid the temptation: "Even if these exaggerated shapes looked smart or attractive and even if they didn't ruin pretty, healthy feet, it would still be silly to choose them." [xlv] Similarly Eileen Allen in

opposite **The associated problems of the stiletto heel occupied designers across the world. Sold as "floor friendly," these stilettos with detachable blunt tips were designed in Stuttgart, Germany, by Wolfgang Schmidt in 1962.**

below **The original Gina wheel stiletto of 1962 was designed by Mehmet Kurdash to prevent steel-tipped heels destroying parquet flooring.**

The Book of Beauty (1961) appealed to a woman's vanity: "very high heels etch weary lines on a face, however young, and give older people irritable bouts and headaches. So you can see that your feet, badly shod, may spoil you beautiful nature." xlvi The "needle-needle heel" as it was dubbed in the United States caused a minor revolt in 1961. Abigail Van Buren of "Dear Abby" fame, a syndicated column across the States, sent an open letter to the National Shoe Manufacturers' Association with 100,000 letters from women to back her up: "Please do what you can, when you can, gentlemen, to liberate the captive feet of womanhood. It's not fair and it's not fun to hurt from the ground up in the name of fashion." xlvii It would be disingenuous to say that the stiletto heel caused no foot problems at all – many women to this day have the bunions to prove otherwise. However, it was the vehemence of the attacks that shows the cultural fear of a woman displaying sex so openly, and through wearing objects that had such a penetrative quality to them.

Women were quite literally making their mark on culture. For by the early 1960s all museums, galleries, and historic country houses had called a ban on the stiletto because of the damage it was wreaking on their wooden floors. A new public sign even had to be invented – the cancelled-out stiletto shoe. As fashion historian David Kunzle remembers,

"The more enterprising flooring manufacturers meanwhile saw the stiletto as a challenge. An architect told me that this fashion was the best thing to happen in years to the flooring industry, without it certain synthetics marketed in the 1960s might never have become generally available." xlviii

In 1962 the British National Coal Board announced the "End of the Stiletto Vendetta" with an advert promoting Armourtile flooring's capacity to resist

"the trail of destruction left in the fashionable wake of women. 1 ton of female – the average impact of the

right *By the 1960s, the image of the stiletto was one of sexuality mixed with danger. The heel could, quite literally, prove a weapon in the battle of the sexes.*

stiletto heel is the lacerating, splintering, tearing scourge that confronts the floor-covering industry. If she pirouettes, the effect would be comparable with that of a heavy power drill of the type used in mining or quarrying." xlvix

One 1950s teenager recalls a christening in 1960, after which a newly veneered sapele floor had to be re-covered with a new carpet after suffering so much damage from the stiletto heel. Could it get any worse? Yes, according to one newspaper in 1958: "Women's stiletto heeled shoes are blamed for breaking up roads in Carshalton, Surrey." l

Luckily Mehmet Kurdash of Gina shoes had found a solution. In 1962 he designed a stiletto with a precision-made steel wheel on the tip of a truncated tapered heel, asserting:

"This is meant as a serious alternative to small-based heels which have been banned from dance halls, churches, and schools because they damage floors … The disc is set at a critical angle, so that as the wearer puts her foot on it a brake action is achieved. On completion of the walking movement, the disc is given a slight turn, so that a new surface is continually applied as the walker progresses." li

By the mid-1960s the stiletto shoe had become a mainstream teenage fashion, no longer representing the *haute couture* chic of Paris or the cool modernity of Italy. It was part of the new pop culture, a sexy glamour-girl look inspired by Hollywood and worn by millions. And by 1965 women were thinking better of this now fully established shoe fashion. Running off almost daily to the local heel bar to have the heel tip replaced was something of a chore and the thin heels could get scuffed by the smallest holes in pavements. By 1965 the stiletto had had its day, replaced by the new flatties, which seemed to represent a new decade and a newly liberated, androgynous image for young women. The stiletto was to go underground, to emerge later stronger, leaner, and faster than ever before.

WICKED...
ELEGANT
Airborne
PARIS POINTS

SPIKES AND LASHES

"The modern Amazon shoots arrows

into the ground with her feet, and strikes

two-fold pleasure-pain, imagined or real,

into the fantasy of the male."

Cecil Willet-Cunningham [i]

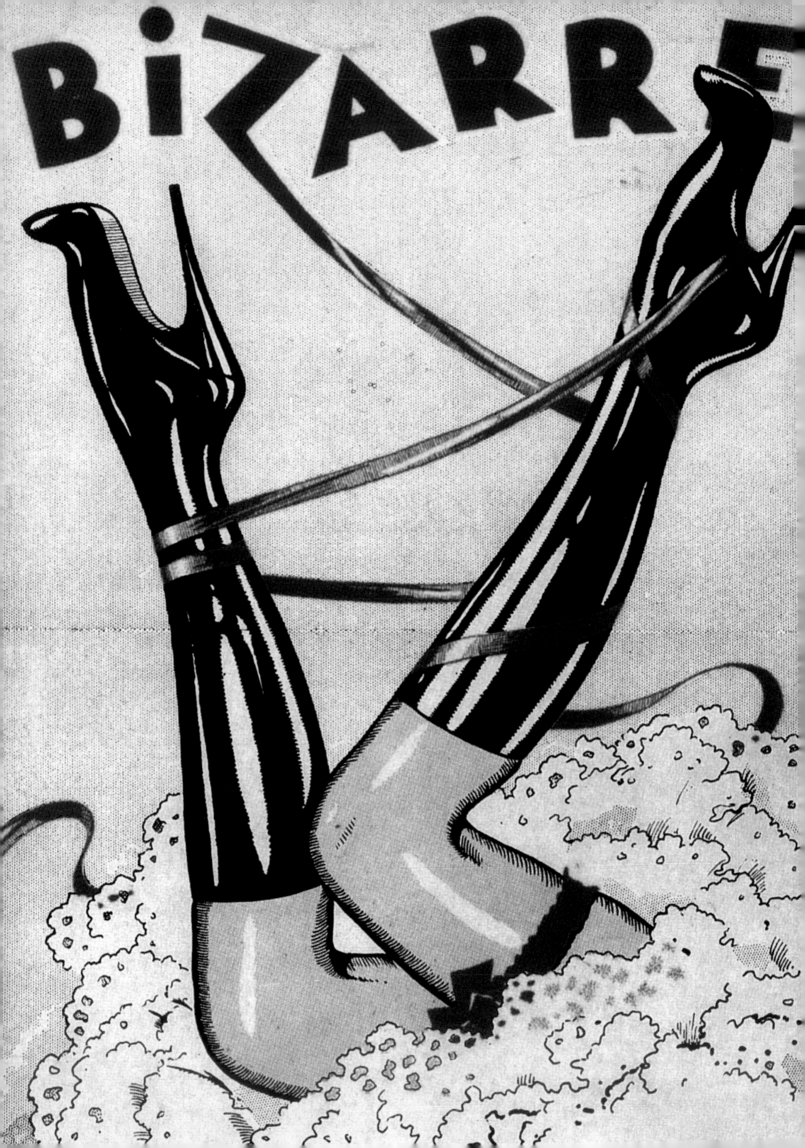

previous page *Guy West of Jeffrey West shoes has designed the ultimate stiletto (c.2000), wittily harking back to its linguistic roots as the razor-sharp Italian knife.*

opposite *John Willie's* Bizarre *magazine of the 1950s often covered foot and shoe fetishism. This cover illustration of 1952 mixes bondage, water play, and the appeal of the knee-length, stiletto-heeled boot.*

below *An image from* Bizarre, *1946. In this period, the tight-laced corset had disappeared from mainstream fashion to go underground – when worn with a pair of high stiletto heels, it became a popular fetish fashion.*

The stiletto heel inspires abject devotion. It rivals the erotic power of the wearer's naked body by sending out a heady mix of sexual signals. It can be dominating and phallic – a "bitchy pump" – but at the same time hobbling and passive, the reading dependent on the viewer or the wearer. Its very design arches the insole and shortens the foot. The combination of high, hardened heel with an ankle in a permanently flexed state effects a magical transformation – the stiletto shoe, the pre-eminent symbol of femininity evokes the erect penis. It is the ultimate fetish. It is not surprising, therefore, that the first true stilettos existed in sado-masochistic pornography before they entered into the fashion system in the 1950s, then conjured up in the fevered imagination of the fetishist for his own sexual pleasure.

In the early twentieth century the psychoanalyst Sigmund Freud (1856–1939) described how a fetish object could result when a male child recognized the absence of a penis in his mother during his early sexual development. Fearing the possibility of his own castration – if it has happened to his mother, then it could happen to him – he invents a surrogate, which becomes the fetish object without which his pleasure is beset by anxiety. ii For the writer Rétif de la Bretonne (1734–1806) it is the shoe that becomes a substitute for the corporeal presence of his lover, Colette,

"Dragged away from the stormiest, completely adoring passion for Colette, I imagined seeing and feeling her in body and spirit by caressing the shoes she had worn just a moment ago with my hands. I pressed my lips on one of the jewels while the other substituted as woman during a frenzied fit … this bizarre, mad pleasure seemed to – how should I say? – seemed to lead me straight to Colette herself." iii

Colette's shoes inspire sexual passion, fetishistic surrogates relating back to the moment in infancy when, according to Freud, de la Bretonne would have

recognized his mother's lack of phallus. As Gilles Deleuze (1925–95) explains in *Masochism* (1991),

"The constant return to this object … enables him to validate the existence of the organ … in dispute. The fetish is therefore not a symbol at all, but … a frozen, arrested, two-dimensional image, a photograph to which one returns repeatedly to exorcise the dangerous consequences of movement, the harmful discoveries that result from exploration …" [iv]

The fetish becomes the woman's penis that, as Freud put it, "the little boy does not want to give up," [v] is determined still to believe in, and is ultimately decided by the last object he saw as an infant before becoming aware of his mother's supposed castration. De la Bretonne's choice of shoe is common for, as Freud explains, it is the object most usually glimpsed by a boy beneath his mother's skirts as he inquisitively peers up at her genitals. [vi] The shoe becomes a tantalizing talisman and its accidental exposure causes a man's heart to race – especially during historical periods when the revealing of a foot and leg beneath fashionably long skirts was somewhat of a taboo. Hence the incidence and subsequent documentation of foot and shoe fetishism in the nineteenth century.

One of the first psychological case histories examining sexual fetishism was the *Psychopatha Sexualis* of 1886 by Richard von Kraft-Ebbing (1840–1902). It includes the story of "Z," age 28, who "at the age of thirteen developed a weakness for ladies' boots with high heels;" [vii] and "Mr X," who had recurring "dreams at night made up of shop scenes: either I stand before the window of a shoe shop regarding the elegant ladies' shoes – particularly buttoned shoes – or I lie at a lady's feet and smell and lick her shoes," [viii] A more recent foot fetishist surfaces in Geoff Nicholson's *Footsucker* of 1995, where the narrator looks unashamedly at women and their feet,

"and every so often I'd do something a little bit eccentric. I'd hang around outside women's shoe

Strange Hungers

FN 101

75¢

ADULTS
ONLY

by
RICHARD
POLK

THIS IS AN ORIGINAL FN NITER

for slaves of fashion

Achilles

theatrical footwear

shops, looking at the shoes in the window and looking through into the store at the women putting shoes on and taking them off. And once in a while I'd spot a great looking pair of feet walking along the street and I'd follow them for a couple of miles." [ix]

What constitutes the most lickable foot and shoe has been debated for generations, but across history and culture particular features recur. The foot should be dainty, perfectly formed, and, for many, tightly shod. The infamous bound foot of Imperial China, for instance, played an important part in linking the foot and shoe with the carnal and can only be described as a cultural fixation. The "lotus foot" was the principal focus of male sexual ecstasy from the tenth to the early twentieth centuries, created by binding the foot of a female child from the age of five tightly from back to front with the four smaller toes pushed down under the ball of the foot. The forefoot and heel were then pushed together and securely bound until the bones had gradually ossified into place by the age of about eighteen. The tightly constrained lotus foot was considered the epitome of femininity, used in sexual games as both a phallic stimulant and substitute. It was lyrically described as having "divine quality" and "seductive attitude" and a mere glimpse could have men in raptures. Some tiny shoes, fashioned by the women themselves, have tooth marks in them after having been bitten during a night of passion.

The tiny foot was also a symbol of social status, denoting an aristocratic lifestyle that marked one out from the labouring peasant classes, with their broad, unrestricted feet. *Footsucker* also details psychologists Arline and John Liggett describing how,

"Husbands were unanimous in their conviction that the tiny-footed woman made the best bedmate. Even apart from love-making, if she placed herself against you when you slept, you did not feel a heavy weight, and this was most agreeable. A large-footed woman moving under the bedclothes was less desirable as she could cause an annoying draught of cold air." [x]

opposite *The ankle strap of these 1970s red patent-leather fetish heels photographed by Colin Robinson creates a shackling effect reminiscent of prisoners in a chain gang.*

below *The cautionary tale of* The Red Shoes *by Hans Christian Andersen warned children of the dangers of vanity. Thinking of nothing but the red shoes she wears to church, Karen displays a resistance to God that leads to an appalling punishment.*

What is more, she was mocked with names such as "duckfoot" or "lotus boat." The bound foot was thus the most extreme embodiment of podic beauty by being both petite and elegantly arched, and inspiring love at first sight. In Western culture the diminutive *pied* can also spark the same intensity of feeling. In the celebrated erotic novel of 1886, *Venus in Furs* by Leopold von Sacher-Masoch (1836–95), the narrator Severin is overcome with lust at the sight of Wanda and falls to the ground in a fit of passion:

"I was on my knees before her and pressing my burning face into the perfumed muslin of her dress. 'Severin, you should not do that.' Nevertheless I seized her dainty foot and kissed it. 'You are getting more and more out of hand!' she exclaimed. Tearing herself out of my grasp she fled toward the house, while her delicate slipper remained in my hands." [xi]

This exquisite beauty has to be accompanied by pain, however, and the classic fairytale *The Red Shoes* in a version by Hans Christian Andersen (1805–75) demonstrates, in a tale of religious morality, the beautiful shoe's relationship with cruelty. Karen, an early example of fashion victim, dares to wear a pair of red dancing shoes for her confirmation and, seduced by their beauty, fails to remember her prayers. On leaving church she begins to dance and cannot stop:

"She was very much frightened and tried to throw off her red shoes, but could not unclasp them. She hastily tore off her stockings; but the shoes she could not get rid of – they had, it seemed, grown on to her feet. Dance she did, and dance she must, over field and meadow, in rain and in sunshine, by night and by day; the shoes bore her continually over thorns and briars, till her limbs were torn and bleeding." [xii]

The only recourse from shoes that were quite literally killing her is to persuade a woodcutter to chop off her feet, "but even after this the shoes still danced away with those little feet over the fields, and into the deep forests." [xiii] This traditional tale reappears consistently in various guises in fetish

right *The associations of pain,
pleasure, and women's shoes are
laid bare in the traditional fairytale
of Cinderella. In original versions
of the tale, the ugly sisters hacked
off their toes so they could fit their
feet into the tiny glass slipper.*

magazines from the early twentieth century
onward, in versions such as *The Stiletto Trap* of
2003, an urban folk tale for a new generation:

"I … found a pair of black patent pumps with 5in
[12cm] heels, the bottom half a gold metallic spike …
the metal heels tapered to a point about ⅛in [0.3cm]
in diameter … I slid the [shoes] on and stood up …
as I walked towards the mirror, I heard a small click
and pop from each shoe and felt something …
wrapping around my toes tightly … The shoes
were on my feet to stay." [xiv]

After trying to remove the shoes with a wrench, a
blow torch, and an electric bolt cutter, the victim
has to learn to walk, run, swim, and ride a bike in the
stiletto heels enduring much discomfort until "A year
had passed since the day it all started. I didn't even
notice the heels any more. I have adjusted." [xv]

The tale of Cinderella (alluded to in Sacher-Masoch's
Venus in Furs [1870] in Wanda's adandonment of
her slipper) follows the pain-pleasure script. By her
virtue, purity, and aristocracy Cinderella's tiny foot
fits snugly into the elegant glass slipper, "that tiny
receptacle into which some part of the body can slip
and fit tightly," [xvi] as Bruno Bettelheim (1903–90)
puts it in his psychological interpretation of
fairytales. In Grimm's account, the large ugly feet
of her sisters can't fit into the glass shoe – if they
persist they will cause it to shatter – and so they
are prepared to cut off their toes to win the hand of
the handsome prince. On the sidelines their mother
shouts encouragement: "Cut off your toes! When you
are Queen, you won't have to walk any more." [xvii]
(A bizarre 1950s version of the tale describes a top
model of the day, Barbara Goalen, as having both her
little toes amputated in a bid to squeeze into the
slenderest winklepicker shoe.)

Sacher-Masoch is also responsible for adding the lash
of the whip into this heady mix, as the libertine Severin
persuades his lover Wanda to engage, not just with his
love of the shoe, but with his love of flagellation:

"'You drive me to distraction!'
She gives a slight pout of contempt and looks at me with narrowed, mocking eyes.
'Give me the whip.'
I look about the room.
'No,' she cries, 'stay on your knees.' She … takes the whip off the ledge and, watching me with a smile, makes it whistle through the air …" xviii

This early example of a whip-wielding dominatrix, in turn inspired by the sexual fantasies of the Marquis de Sade (1740–1814), is a model on which many later images are based. The pleasure-pain combination in this kind of sexual role-play is given added *frisson* with clothing that constricts the body while exaggerating its sexual zones. High heels enter the slave-mistress's wardrobe in the 1890s when "staggerers" or boudoir shoes were used for pleasures of polymorphous perversity. Based on a romantic fantasy of a seventeenth-century Cromwell shoe, the staggerer could only be worn at home; it was impossible to walk in, but provided the most petite of silhouettes when peeping slyly from the m'lady's skirts. But it is really in the late 1930s that the sadistic vixen clad in tight-laced leather corset and killer heels with a whip to discipline and punish is fully established as a popular stereotype of femininity within the fetish underground. Magazines such as *London Life* and *Bizarre*, which under the helm of the fetish photographer John Willie (1902–62) ran from 1946 to 1956, acknowledged the power of high heels when worn by a dangerous *femme fatale*.

Together with the increased height given by a 15cm (6in) spike heel, a woman could prove to be an untouchable object. With a hardened, phallic body that inspired both terror and sexual longing, the trampling harridan in leather, pin heels, and wielding a whip can be seen in the work of illustrator Eric Stanton (1926–99) who specialized in images of power-crazed women trampling on slave males. The heel as a sleek, hard-edged weapon also appears in popular pulp fiction and in the more hardcore shoe fetish magazines such as *Fantastique* and *Exotique*,

both published in the 1950s, which contained narratives
of dominance and submission. In this extract from the
pulp novel *Rue Marquis de Sade* by Morgana Baron
(1996), the erotics of the stiletto are made clear:

"The leather was tightened over Charlotte's straining
instep until both creaked ... Being compressed to
permanent *en pointe*, her size-four [US size 6.5] foot
seemed to have tapered away to almost nothing. The
curve of her arch was now dramatically erotic. Her
ankle, always slender, now looked fragile enough to
snap at the least strain. The stiletto was a thin spike,
vicious as a dagger, extending past her heel to a
needle point." xix

Here the stiletto compresses the foot into the ideal
shape by exaggerating the arch and ankle, while
at the same time restricting the body's movement.
By arching the foot in such an exaggerated way,
allusions are made to the natural reflex of the foot
and toes that Alfred Kinsey (1894–1956), in his
research into the sexual modes and mores of the
American woman in the 1950s, observed occurring
during orgasm. The teetering, wobbling gait caused
by attempts to balance on a needle point also
promotes an exaggerated change in posture.
According to Paula Sanchez, who wrote for *Bizarre*
magazine in the 1950s,

"The slight jar produced by extra-high heels results
in an eye-catching quivering wave in the plump
protruding breasts ... There is an alternate side-to-
side movement of the hips, a sway in the direction
of whichever foot appears to be carrying the weight ...
this hula-like movement becomes automatic ... and
the tighter the corset, the more emphatic becomes
this movement of the derrière." xx

When the points of the heel are at their smallest, the
support for the heel is drastically reduced. The ankle
has to then take compensatory action leading to a
"lateral quiver," as David Kunzle puts it in *Fashion
and Fetishism* (1982), which may be interpreted by men
as a sexual solicitation. The silhouette of the stiletto

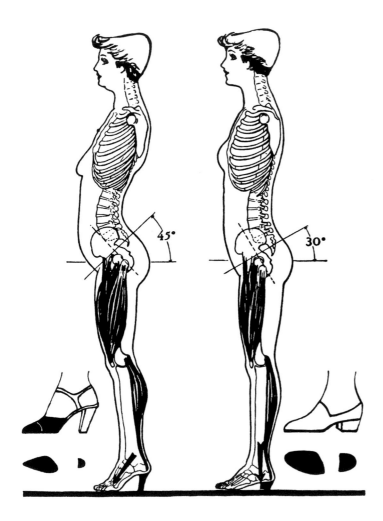

wearer becomes unmistakably female. Its very design limits the range of action in the foot and restricts the walk of the wearer, while at the same time it pushes the body into a most alluring feminine shape with breasts thrust out and bottom behind for balance. The 15cm (6in) heels give extra height and thus increased psychological power. The rather frightening dominance of this figure has a sweetener, though – the idea that women are more sexually responsive in stilettos. The restricted walk that stilettos encourage is commonly believed to promote physiological changes in a woman's sexual organs by increasing the muscle power of the vagina while at the same time enlarging the muscles in the buttocks. This generates pleasure in both the wearer and the viewer. One stiletto wearer remarked,

"I feel as if I am in a constant state of tension, simply standing, I am on the go, turning around, bending to file a paper, is a balancing act; I am at rest only when I sit, which is never for long. I wear these heels because they make me feel in constant contact with my body." xxi

And the story of "Mollie" that appeared in a fetish magazine in the mid-1950s written by David Kunzle describes her footwear and its associated gait in detail:

"The heels varied in height from 4in [10cm] to 7½in [19cm] and the shoes were mainly black patent courts. The most thrilling pair with the 7½in [19cm] heels were in a sort of dull kid in gray with gold heels, very thin and spiky – when wearing these Mollie … tripped about with a most fascinating wiggle of the hips and sway of her breasts." xxii

Mollie's "fascinating wiggle" epitomizes the draw of the heel. And it is this walk that is interpreted as an open sexual invitation by men, and is a lure used by the lurking dominatrix. Therein lies the pleasure and danger of the stiletto, making a woman at once submissive and aggressive, fetish and fetishist, both predator and prey. As William Rossi, the podiatrist and footwear historian, concurs,

The "6" inch Heel ___

fig ①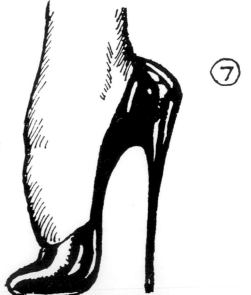

②

$6''$

$\overset{\times}{\underset{A}{\mid}} \overset{}{\underset{}{\leftarrow 3'' \rightarrow}} \overset{}{\underset{B}{\mid}}$ $\underset{D}{\cdot}$

$\overset{}{\underset{A}{\mid}} \leftarrow 3'' \overset{\times}{\underset{B}{\mid}}$ $6''$ $\overset{}{\underset{C \cdot D}{\mid}}$

Elementary mathematics

③ $5''$ heel

$6''$

$\overset{}{\underset{A}{\mid}} \overset{\times}{\underset{B}{\mid}} \overset{}{\underset{}{3''}} \overset{}{\underset{D}{\mid}}$
3·33" (approx)

④ $6''$ heel

$6''$

$\overset{}{\underset{A}{\mid}} \overset{}{\underset{B}{\mid}} \overset{}{\underset{D}{\mid}}$
$3''$

⑤

$4\tfrac{3}{4}''$ Heel

⑥

shaded portions are empty space

6
5
4
3
2
1

⑦

$6''$ Heel

how the impossible is made possible for the average foot.

which by its very nature condemned women as mere decoration, and contributors to a system of false needs. Fashion was believed to be an expression of female subordination that was masquerading as personal choice. Women, on entering the fashion system through consumer spending, were exhibiting false consciousness. As one popular feminist chant of the late 1960s and early '70s proclaimed, "Fashion = control = violence against women." New forms of dress were constructed emphasizing practicality and utility, and therefore use before beauty. Women were no longer prepared to be mere sex objects, existing only for the gratification of the greedy male gaze. Joan Cassell, feminist anthropologist and writer, describes an early feminist meeting where the feminist contingent,

"wore jeans or denim workmen's overalls, the baggy kind that hid the shape of the wearer. The pants might be topped by a man's T-shirt or work shirt … footgear was comfortable, with a predominance of heavy men's work boots or sneakers." [xxv]

This was a natural, and supposedly uncorrupted, look. Dolores, the heroine of the 1980s feminist novel *The Bleeding Heart* by Marilyn French, similarly shows her rejection of patriarchal values through her choice of dress by wearing "Indian shirts and jeans, bare feet wherever possible, and never, under any circumstances, high heels." [xxvi]

The stiletto was singled out by early feminists as an example of a fashion that politically oppressed women. Germaine Greer made this clear in *The Female Eunuch*, a textbook for the liberated woman published in 1971, condemning footwear

"which alters all the torsion of the muscles of the thighs and pelvis and throws the spine into an angle which is still in some circles considered essential to allure." [xxvii]

And in America Karen Durbin, in an article for *Ms* magazine in the 1970s, wrote:

"Spike heels are combat boots in a sex war where women are the losers; an emblem of the old-style vamp who telegraphs a hostile eroticism, the futile gesture of the woman whose only weapons are, as venerable fashion parlance has it, a 'drop dead' dress and a stiletto heel." xxviii

The stiletto seemed a literal embodiment of the social shackles imposed on women from birth and preventing them from gaining equality within society, as Susan Brownmiller put it in her book *Femininity* (1984),

"suggestive of the restraining leg irons and ankle chains endured by captive animals, prisoners, and slaves who were also festooned with decorative symbols of their bondage." xxix

In fashion terms, though, the stiletto was to stage a comeback. Fashion photographers began to use the language of sado-masochistic fetishism in their work in the mid- to late 1970s, as it seemed to fit the cocaine-fuelled decadence of disco culture. The heady nightlife of Studio 54 in Manhattan, New York, was described by British journalist Jean Rook as

"a seething pot of smoking, writhing, and dancing bodies, lit up with a massive man-in-the-moon snorting cocaine from a spoon and by strobes that make girls' eyes hang out of their heads like their boobs tumble out of their shirts." xxx

Studio 54 and the Embassy Club in Paris provided apt settings for the louche imagery of photographers Helmut Newton (1920–2004) and Guy Bourdin (1928–91). Their loveless images of cruelty and sophistication graced the pages of all editions of *Vogue* and *Harper's Bazaar*. Bourdin's cutting-edge campaigns for Charles Jourdan are among the most stunning and cruel of that decade, depicting the aftermath of crashes and blood-stained heels that threatened murder of the most brutal kind. In Bourdin's work for Jourdan, the weapon-related sado-masochistic associations of the stiletto were at their most explicit, yet retained an eerie glamour.

below *In 1977, artist Philip Castle created a chimera, half woman and half spider, in his airbrush creation* YB-49. *At the time, Castle's images were read as sexist, but today they have been reinterpreted as powerful images of female sexuality.*

left *Stilettos were revived in high fashion in the 1970s, here worn with new "designer" jeans by Gloria Vanderbilt. Their image became one of decadent disco glamour worn by the likes of model Marie Helvin and socialite Bianca Jagger.*

below *Terry de Havilland was the premier stiletto designer of the 1970s – Cher had 13 pairs. The Zebedee shoe (c.1975) shows his witty glam-rock references and superb craftsmanship.*

A London shoe designer whose stilettos also conjure up this erotomania is Terry de Havilland, who worked for most of the major designers in the 1970s and had Bianca Jagger, Cher, and Bette Midler among his customers. Born Terry Higgins, de Havilland trained at his parents' factory, which produced a myriad styles including the stiletto under the name Waverley Shoes from the 1950s to the 1970s, until the tragic death of his father on the factory premises. De Havilland inherited his father's love of the stiletto, and remembered his almost Pavlovian response on hearing the click-click of a pair of heels on the city pavements: "He would cup his ear and say 'Listen, music!'" xxxi

Terry remained in the shoe trade, becoming a legend in fashion circles and ultimately responsible for the renaissance of the stiletto after years of flat styles in the 1960s and '70s:

"I think I was the person who brought the stiletto back. Zandra Rhodes did a show in the King's Road in the theatre where *The Rocky Horror Show* [sic] was playing and I showed a few at Milan in the early 1970s." xxxii

He underwent opposition outside the fashion circles within which he moved, though:

"I did a show at Olympia and one of the early female television presenters was there. She came on stage

opposite *Punk took the deadly glamour of the stiletto into the city, playing with the trashy look of the "bad girl" and creating an aggressively sexual, yet subversive, image that toyed with traditional ideas of "good taste."*

below *In the UK in 1977, punk stilettos could be ordered from small manufacturers advertising in the* New Musical Express *magazine. Colours included "slash yellow" and "bondage black," both "anarchistically priced."*

with a suit on, 'Don't you know stiletto heels are really bad for women's feet?' 'Yeah, but really good for their heads,' I replied. I was really glad I said that." xxxiii

He believes stilettos are a powerful style for women, "because they're purely about sex, the original f**k-me shoes," xxxiv and has always made libidinous connections in his work to which many have responded – including one surprising name. He recalls a pair of black leather thigh-high boots with a stiletto heel and red satin lining, which were ordered by a customer for her sister in the 1970s:

"It was only when we got the cheque for the deposit and saw the name Princess Lee Radziwill, we realized who her sister was – Jackie Kennedy! The boots were a size 8 [US size 10.5] and we wondered whether they were for her or for Aristotle Onassis himself." xxxv

De Havilland understands the essential appeal of the needle heel. "They'll always be stilettos. They go in and out of fashion, but they're always in style." xxxvi His career trajectory shows this, for after moving out of high fashion in the early 1980s he started producing subcultural styles first under the name Kamikaze Shoe "which did a Kamikaze in 1988" xxxvii and then under the name Magic Shoes in response to the demand from both the punk and the goth movements. At one point they were making 800 pairs of shoes a day, for young women were now subverting the cultural meanings of the stiletto.

Punk women, fetish fantasies made flesh, had stalked out of the pages of pornography right on to the city streets. The image of the dominatrix had been reclaimed and men, who were used to consuming her with subterfuge in the privacy of their own homes, on their own terms, suddenly were no longer in control. Punks took the language of sexual fetishism and used it for their own ends – rubber and leather, fishnet stockings, and winklepicker stilettos. Defiant stares, black eyeliner, and killer heels were used to construct an image that

The British designer Vivienne Westwood here incorporated the spike heel into a work that often refers to its Punkish origins. In this black-and-white example, the power of the heel as a deadly weapon in the battle of the sexes cannot be missed.

Work "Ball Desire" created by [illegible]-inspired Colin Robinson in 2001, a contemporary triptych using vintage fetish heels. The space created by the silhouette of the heel evokes the painting.

was deviant, perverse, threatening, and tribal. In America the look was championed by Debbie Harry whose brash glamour band The Stilettos mutated into Blondie by the mid-1970s. For most, though, conventional prettiness was spat on – punk women were not going to behave. Style writer Peter York describes a scene he witnessed outside London's Roxy Club in 1977:

"In would go ordinary little girls, carrying bags containing make-up and safety pins: out would come Monsterettes, street vixens: crop-haired toughies apparently on parole from the remand home; Rocky Horrors in fishnet and stilettos and black knickers. The girls would then dance together, grappling like baby psychopaths." xxxvii

Vivienne Westwood, fashion designer and doyenne of punk, made the relationship between street style and fetishism clear with her Bondage Collection of 1976. Inspired by Louise's, a Soho sex club frequented by strippers, drag artists, and bondage freaks, Westwood used straps, buckles, leather, and leopardskin stilettos to create clothes that shocked middle England, announcing that "sex is the thing that bugs English people more than anything else, so that's where to attack." xxxix Parents were appalled at daughters who, instead of aping Farrah Fawcett-Majors' *Charlie's Angels* flicks, were now cutting their own hair, bleaching it white, and wearing spiked heels – an image usually associated with the local prostitute. But these girls weren't for sale: quite the reverse. In fact, as they were in charge of their own pleasures. In 1977, fashion anthropologist Ted Polhemus documented the scene for British *Vogue*, describing a punk girl in a club near Oxford Street:

"A red light shines on a girl with fluorescent orange hair. Her face is chalk white and her eye sockets blackened. She is wearing a black leather dog collar and studded wristbands. Her T-shirt is adorned with metal chains and zips and ... her skin has been replaced with black PVC, terminating in ice-pink stilettos." xl

left *Fetish references had crossed over into mainstream fashion by the 1980s. Here, fetish clothiers Ectomorph show an alternative mode of power dressing using rubber and high heels.*

By the 1980s, through the mainstreaming of punk style, fetishism had entered mainstream fashion in a myriad ways. The relationship between power, control, and gender was being debated at the highest levels with the emergence of Margaret Thatcher as the first female prime minister of Britain, and more and more women were beginning to enter that bastion of male power, the executive arena. But what was the new woman boss to wear? John T. Molloy understood the dilemma and gave voice to women's fears in his manual of 1980, *Women: Dress For Success.* He described a luncheon appointment with some major players in a business consortium. After arriving at the assigned meeting place and not seeing any likely clients he had them paged, after which he,

"discovered to my embarrassment that they were sitting less than 10ft [3 m] away. They were three of the best and most conservatively dressed women I had ever met, yet I had never considered the possibility that they might be my executives. I had been looking for three men." xli

This, perhaps, says much about Molloy's prejudices, but his manual hit a nerve and was a resounding success. He prescribed a diet of serious, sober suiting in the restrained colours of grey, medium blue, and beige for women so they could blend into a male environment. Pastels, particularly pink and pale yellow, were to be avoided:

"Businesswomen cannot get away with wearing feminine prints with flowers, birds, sail boats, and the like. Although most of these prints are perfectly acceptable to wear socially, they will make men think that a businesswoman wearing them to work is frilly and ineffective." xlii

And, of course, he had much to say about shoes;

"the best shoe for the businesswoman is the plain pump, in a dark colour, with closed toe and heel. The heel should be 1½in [4cm] high. Women have five times as many foot problems as men. That is because

opposite **A Charles Jourdan stiletto heel of the 1980s in red suede. The adjustment from dominatrix to power dresser is made clear in this image of high-fashion femininity.**

below **The rise of women in the executive arena in the 1980s led to the stereotype of the female executive as dominatrix, most notably in the shape of Cameron Cook, the anti-heroine of Jilly Cooper's book** Rivals.

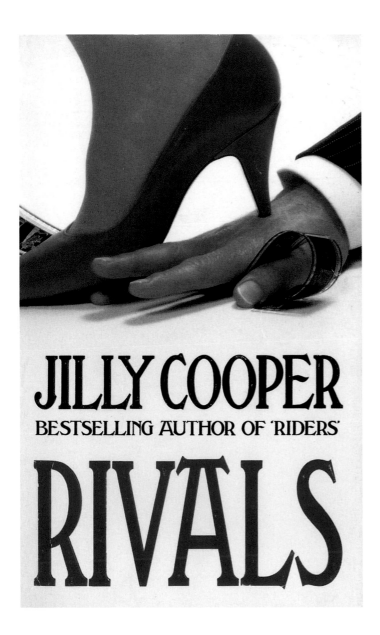

they wear imported trash on their feet. Two groups are getting rich on this: the retailers and the foot doctors. The women who are being crippled are taking a beating." xliii

This look, called "dress for success" in the States, was soon dubbed "power dressing" across the world. Women leaving Harvard Business School, for instance, were advised to wear black or navy suits. Sharply tailored suits with padded shoulders and crisp shirts were worn, and an almost masculinized silhouette became *de rigueur*. However, two features crept in as the 1980s progressed, of which Molloy thoroughly disapproved: the short skirt and the spiked heel. Journalist Charlotte du Cann described this subversion of Molloy's dictates in *Thatcherstyle* (1989): "Even those who only once wore difficult statements in black by Japanese designers suddenly wanted … a simple, direct Chanel suit and high heels." xliv

Thus a new dominatrix was born, the ball-busting female executive with a drive for power, exceeded only by that of her sexuality. In her 1982 ubiquitous shopping and f***king novel, *Lace*, Shirley Conran conveys perfectly the interplay of power and sex between the main characters:

"Before Griffin realized what she was doing she'd slashed through the jacket of his handmade suit. She started to snip through his silk shirt, imported the previous month from Jermyn Street. She put the shears down, picked up her tights, stuffed them in his mouth, and gagged him with his thin silk tie. Then she carefully slashed up the other trouser leg and yanked away the debris of grey flannel." xlv

The business Amazon with her hardened, gym-honed body wearing metropolitan chic as some form of modern body armour is similarly embodied in the steely character of Cameron Cook in Jilly Cooper's *Rivals* of 1988, whose cover shows a high-heeled shoe grinding into the hand of a clearly impotent male. Wearing high-fashion fetishism in her "extremely tight-fitting, strapless, black-studded dress which

left *American actress Heather Locklear in stiletto heels and fishnets. In the 1980s, American soap operas such as* Dallas *and* Dynasty *promoted this type of overtly sexual look.*

came 8in [20cm] above her knees," [xlvi] Cameron Cook is described in one scene as

"lounging menacingly by the window, wearing a black polo neck, black leather trousers, and spiky high heels. Declan wondered if she walked all over Tony in them." [xlvii]

Perhaps the fear engendered by this strident figure can be seen in the portrayal of the modern yuppies, or in this case vamps, who crowd the pages of Anne Billson's 1993 modern horror novel *Suckers*. In the setting of the chic glass towers of London's Docklands, Dora, a "hard-nosed and cynical creative consultant," [xlviii] begins to witness killings – but not of the financial kind. A vampire, Lulu, has become the new face for the perfume Kuroi and is introduced in an advert (obviously parodying the style of the time – just think of Calvin Klein's perfume, Obsession) as

"a figure, dressed in black, stalking down a neon-lit street in ridiculously high heels. The other pedestrians, all male, were going ape-shit. The first gulped down a lethal dose of strychnine – you knew it was strychnine because it said so on the bottle. The second threw himself under the wheels of a Ferrari. The third plunged a knife into his belly, and the fourth was so traumatized his head exploded." [xlix]

In one of the final scenes of *Suckers*, Dora grapples with Lulu in the bathroom, and her stilettos prove to be her undoing:

"I ... grabbed the edge of the mat and tugged it up as hard as I could. If she'd been wearing sensible footwear she'd have regained her balance easily. But ... she was wearing flamboyant f***-me shoes with lizard-skin trimming and 4in [10cm] spikes. So when the earth moved beneath her feet she teetered back and forth ..., the rim of the bath caught her behind the knees and she landed in the water with her legs in the air." [l]

The language of fetish dress had become socially acceptable by the 1980s and the figure of the female

executive as dominatrix held sway right through that decade and into the 1990s, appearing in international high-gloss soap operas such as *Dallas* and *Dynasty* and the catwalk looks of Thierry Mugler, Nick Coleman, and Pam Hogg. Even the white stiletto of the 1960s underwent a resurgence on the back of the British Mod revival and Two Tone movement in the early 1980s, but its subsequent popularity made it one of the most reviled shoes of the twentieth century. Too many girls wore white stilettos and too many cheap and nasty ones were manufactured to keep up with the demand. The stereotype of the "Essex girl" emerged – a British version of white trailer trash – who had permed and blonded hair, a lycra miniskirt, and dodgy shoes. In this extract from a 1980s poem by Eileen McAuley, "The Seduction: A Clumsy Poem of Teenage Angst," she makes the connection between the glamour of the white stiletto and the tawdry reality of a teenager's life in Birkenhead, England:

"When she discovered she was three months gone,
She sobbed in the cool, locked darkness of her room
And ripped up all her *My Guy* and *Jackie* photo-comics
Until they were just bright paper, like confetti, strewn
On the carpet. And on that day, she broke the heels
Of her high, white shoes (as she flung them at the wall).
And realized, for once, that she was truly frightened
But, more than that, cheated by the promise of it all." [li]

As style writer Peter York put it in his book *Peter York's The Eighties*, "We wanted that power-outfit look, that killer-bimbo look." [lii] The stiletto shoe could accommodate both of these 1980s notions of femininity and cross all classes and professions. The high-heeled shoe had staged an enormous comeback, with the stiletto being one of its many forms: Louis heels, cone shapes, and spikes – it didn't matter as long as it was high and designer: Charles Jourdan, Manolo Blahnik, Andrea Pfister, Maud Frizon, and the more humble Freeman Hardy and Willis. The stiletto had reappeared stronger than ever, and was to dominate fashionable footwear for a new generation.

BALANCING ACT

"Leopard-skin stiletto sandals ... They are the Eartha Kitt of footwear. So sexy they growl. They probably sneak out when I'm at work and lie on the sofa drinking Campari and listening to Peggy Lee."

Maggie Alderson [i]

In the American lifestyle magazine *George*, founded by the late John F. Kennedy Jnr, August 2000, the term "stiletto feminist" was coined for a woman who "embraces easy expressions of sexuality that enhance, rather than detract from, women's freedom." [ii] That same year, Al Gore, Vice-President to Bill Clinton, appeared on *The Oprah Winfrey Show* and complimented the hostess on her stiletto-heeled boots. Manolo Blahnik, designer of sublime stilettos, was also repeatedly name-checked throughout the 1990s on the British comedy series *Absolutely Fabulous*. The stiletto appeared to be undergoing a tremendous renaissance, mirroring women's new feelings of sexual freedom and power. No longer associated with cocktail waitresses and bunny girls, sky-high skinny heels were being paraded by the strongest of women, successful in both executive and sexual arenas – just think of Carrie Bradshaw in *Sex and the City*. In the television series, which first aired in 1998, four independent, successful career women dressed up to the nines and horny as hell, showed you could work hard, play hard, and still look good. In one, now legendary, episode Carrie, played by Sarah Jessica Parker, prizes her heels so highly that while being mugged is heard to wail, "You can take my Fendi baguette, you can take my watch, but don't take my Manolos. I got them half price in a sample sale!" [iii] Later she commands the detective to arrest any woman wearing last season's Blahnik sandals in pink suede.

How had this come to pass? For in the early 1990s the trappings of luxurious femininity were anathema in a new era that seemed to be heralding a change in consciousness – spirituality, sensitivity, and eco-awareness rather than sex and shopping. Fashion appeared to be suffering a momentary schizophrenia. How could a medium that operated on the basis of novelty for novelty's sake, with seasonal changes designed to make perfectly wearable clothes outmoded, fit with the New Age "green-ness" and mania for recycling that was dominating the world's press? How could a woman remain glamorously fashionable, yet ethically and environmentally aware? The answer was "grunge," a look derived from the American rock scene of Seattle, as popularized by the band Nirvana.

previous page Fuchsia-pink heels with ankle ties by Antonio Berardi for his Spring/Summer 2004 ready-to-wear show. In the twenty-first century, catwalk designers have rediscovered the power of the stiletto.

right The four stars of the television series Sex and the City, *Miranda, Charlotte, Carrie, and Samantha, search for Mr Right in a New York populated with "toxic bachelors and 'modelizers.'" Styled by Patricia Field, stilettos were used to symbolize the characters' sexual power and their independence.*

below Since Sex and the City *was first shown in 1998 on American channel HBO, it has been incredibly popular among women, with its mix of sexual mores and fashion, as well as Blahnik heels.*

MANOLO BLAHNIK

left *In the 1980s and '90s, Madonna's style statements incorporated traditionally sexy garments, such as corsets and high heels, which she used to represent a woman in control of her sexuality rather than one stereotyped as a male sex object.*

For men, grunge was flannel work shirts, jeans, and boots; for women a wickedly ironic look dubbed "kinderwhore" by its foremost proponent, musician Courtney Love (and wife of Nirvana frontman Kurt Cobain). Love's subversive style began to seep slowly into high fashion in the early 1990s, with its combination of old-school punk, ripped and customized 1980s tea dresses, smeared red lipstick, and fishnets worn with Doctor Marten boots. This subversion of Hollywood glamour owed much to the pop icon Madonna and her experimentation with dress and female sexual independence in the 1980s. With its heavy drug references and rock-chick belligerence, however, Love's version had a more powerfully dangerous edge. Her inversion of feminine glamour and its use as a weapon, rather than as the sexual objectification of women, informed much of 1990s fashion; within it, one can see the roots of the change in attitude to the stiletto.

In the early 1990s, many women were still ambivalent about the idea of sexualized dressing, fearing being taken as an airhead at work and as a sex object ripe for exploitation when at play. How should one dress in the battle of the sexes? Feminism didn't have much to offer here, having done little to move away from its antipathy to fashion. For women wanting to dress up, feminism was a dirty word. Demonstration dress, the anti-fashion style favoured by radical feminists, had remained stable for too long and had lost its political bite. Conversely, it had contributed to a feeling of alienation among young women wanting to experiment with their appearance rather than being, in Shelagh Young's words, "drab, dungareed dykes whose most playful pastime consists of peering into her friend's vagina with a homemade speculum." iv Gill Hudson, editor of *Company* magazine, commented in 1990,

"they absolutely don't want to be known as feminists ... feminism is not considered sexy ... if we could find a new word and a role-model like Madonna ... it would make the whole thing more attractive to women." v

The new word was, of course, "power" – girl power. Love's look was kidnapped and sanitized by the British

right *The Spice Girls promoted "girl power" in the 1990s – this slogan encapsulated an idea of female solidarity that gave fashion-conscious young women the right to dress as they pleased.*

below *A pair of diamanté-encrusted stilettos by Gina in 2003 evokes a style of 1950s Hollywood glamour, a powerful image of femininity that appeals to many women today.*

pop group The Spice Girls, who came to wide public attention in 1996 and whose cheeky appeal helped to popularize a mass trend toward sexy dressing. Now you could dress in an overtly erotic way, yet still retain your independence. Transformed by "girl power", girls across the world basked in their femininity as shopping was deemed a new, legitimate leisure activity; nail art and body glitter could be discussed at dinner parties, and the Wonderbra became female armour and the mark of a reconstructed feminist. As traditional symbols of femininity such as the push-up bra were being reused to inculcate a powerful post-feminism (think Gossard Wonderbra's "Hello boys" advert of 1994), it wasn't long before the stiletto was rediscovered by a new generation of female consumers. Even staunch feminists were prepared to reassess the stiletto heel. In an article written for *LA Weekly* in 2000, Judith Lewis "reconsidered" the shoe, that "having been banned from the feminist wardrobe had become *de facto* invisible to me." [vi] She continued,

"I do not want my utter disregard for glamour to arouse suspicion when I ask to sample a strappy three-and-a-half incher, DKNY's "sexy" sandal – in silver, no less. I feel almost guilty. There is something decadent about this, something I have determined is *not me* …" [vii]

Her discomfort is increased by a sales assistant who appears instantly to realize her lack of stiletto credentials, emphasizing her conviction that "I am cheating, deceiving, a woman fully and unmistakably inculcated in sensible shoes and I am daring to try on a stiletto heel." [viii] She does, however, discover how a pair of swanky chocolate slingbacks by Max Mara, called Radio, has the potential to change her life:

"By leaving open a deep swath of instep, a high-heeled sandal adds a good 4in [10cm] to a leg. The Radio transformed mine into the stilts of a doll, rendering my bulky calf a hint of shapeliness on an oh-so-slender limb. I am ruined." [ix]

Fashion was fashionable again and style leaders and stiletto feminists such as the formidable journalist Tina

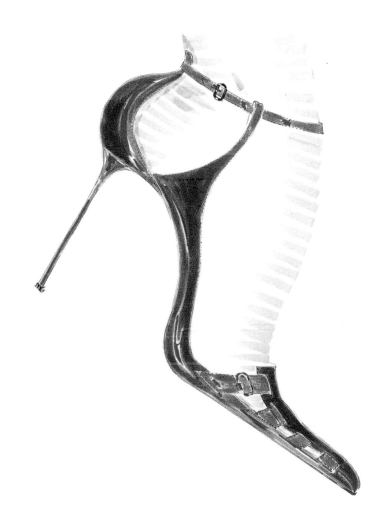

Brown of the *New Yorker* – dubbed "Stalin in high heels" – and Anna Wintour of American *Vogue* traded on the style of the 1980s female executive by combining designer suits with sexy spikes. Wintour and her Manolo Blahniks had been inseparable since the mid-1980s; editor-at-large of American *Vogue*, André Leon Talley, remembers her in 1985 as

"trekking around the cobblestones of London in navy, square-throated, vampy reptile-skin stilettos. They somehow helped to give her an awesome power look that was new." x

With just the right pair of Manolos, Wintour became an object of awe and, in some cases, terror in the fashion world. Writer Toby Young relates a story of her legendary *froideur*, when a senior member of the US *Vogue* staff got her 16-year-old daughter a work placement at the magazine. One day, the girl was walking along a corridor when she saw Wintour approaching. Slightly alarmed, having been warned by her mother of how carefully she must behave in the company of the editor, she continued walking when,

"as they were drawing level, the heel of one of Anna's Manolos snapped and she was sent sprawling to the ground … The girl's first impulse was to ask Anna if she was alright, but then she remembered what her mother had told her: that under no circumstances was she to speak to 'Ms Wintour' – ever. Consequently, she gingerly stepped over Ms Wintour's prostrate form and carried on down the corridor." xi

Once she made her escape, she rushed to her mother's office to ask if she had done the right thing. Her mother assured her categorically that she had.

Wintour wore "limo heels," a term conjured up in the 1990s to describe stiletto shoes that were for women who left the demeaning process of walking to others – they were either too busy or too leisured for it themselves. Physical activity, after all, had its proper place – why else pay all that money for membership of the expensive gym, fitness classes,

opposite *A pair of red stiletto heels by Donna Karan (2000) emerges from a limousine, a perfect illustration of "limo heels", shoes for women who have others to do the walking for them.*

below *Imelda Marcos' shoe collection was discovered in the royal palace after she fled from the Philippines in the 1980s. Her shelves were designed specifically to display each pair of designer heels.*

and personal trainer? The high heel was a mark of conspicuous consumption worn by women who showed their considerable wealth and social status through their feet – these boots were not made for walking. Journalist Tamsin Blanchard described Blahnik's shoes in precisely these terms in *The Shoe: Best Foot Forward*:

"These shoes come with a built-in bill for a … taxi and a driver … They are too good for walking, too grand to risk getting wet in the rain, to push a shopping cart around a supermarket, or to scuff on harsh city streets … they are designed to be worn on antique carpets, or simply dangling from the toes of a fashion editor seated in the front row in a fashion show." [xii]

The relationship between female power and consumer spending (and a certain degree of shoe fetishism) had also been made in the 1980s with the lifestyle of Imelda Marcos, First Lady of the Philippines. Her shoe collection stood as a symbol of her rise from petty middle-class officialdom to a life of luxury as wife of President Ferdinand E. Marcos. Imelda shopped around the world: Harrods of London, Bloomingdales in New York, the rue du Faubourg St. Honoré in Paris, and the via Condotti in Rome. Designers were also summoned to Manila to show off their latest styles for her personal inspection, and one of her favourite firms was Salvatore Ferragamo, then run by his sons Ferruccio and Leonardo. Their father's stiletto designs had been sought out by Marilyn Monroe in the 1950s, but Imelda had enough sway to bring the designers to her on a regular basis. On her flight to exile, she reportedly left behind three thousand pairs of shoes, many personally designed by the Ferragamos, all size 8½ (US size 11), in custom-made racking. "Compared to her, Marie Antoinette was a bag lady," said American congressman Stephen Solarz. [xiii]

Imelda made a fetish of her love of shoes in the 1980s, and by the new millennium the notion of retail therapy – "it's good to shop" – had insidiously worked its way into consumer culture. You are what you buy, and you can buy into the lifestyle of your choosing through your

DONNAKARAN
HOSIERY

INTRODUCING THE ESSENTIALS COLLECTION. INFINITE SHEERS. ULTIMATE OPAQUES. ABSOLUTE LUXURY.

left *These stilettos by Jimmy Choo, designed by Sandra Choi (2003) combine leather and Eastern-inspired jade detail. Choi's designs and Tamara Mellon's astute marketing have placed the company at the forefront of the luxury shoe market in the twenty-first century.*

below *These two delicate shoe designs by Jimmy Choo (2003–4) display the attention to luxurious detailing for which his company is known, along with a high, fine stiletto heel. Choo's shoes are worn by such stars as Charlize Theron, Sharon Stone, and Elizabeth Hurley.*

acquisition of shoes – at least that's what the brand tells us. Due to a canny mix of marketing and celebrity endorsement, the stiletto is no longer a killer heel but a symbol of celebrity status, belying its origins in the fetish fantasies of photographer John Willie and his ilk. One of the most successful shoe companies to rework the image of the needle heel is Jimmy Choo of London and New York. After Princess Diana became one of his customers in the 1990s, the Malaysian-born designer moved from a small atelier in the East End of London to a grand store in Brompton Cross, Chelsea. In 1996 Tamara Mellon, former accessories editor at UK *Vogue*, saw a lucrative business opportunity and bought into the brand. She says,

"Manolo Blahnik was the only competition. That was it. Jimmy was making two pairs of shoes a day by hand from a workshop in the East End. My idea was to take the company to a new level." [xiv]

She and Choo's niece, Sandra Choi, launched a ready-to-wear line with Choi designing and Mellon in charge of business strategy, and in 1998 they opened three outlets in the United States, raising the profile of the brand worldwide. Using herself as the typical customer, Mellon created a shoe with associations of A-list glamour and status. Her looks and luxurious lifestyle and the brand itself have subsequently become fused, a canny strategy that has led to rich rewards. Her business partner, Robert Bensoussan, understands the concept: "It's important to have someone who embodies the brand. People identify with a beautiful woman." [xv] The self-effacing Jimmy Choo, "rarely seen and devoid of Mellon's showmanship," [xvi] according to journalist Claudia Croft, has now been entirely bought out of the brand that bears his name and produces his own Jimmy Choo couture line. The ready-to-wear Choi designs dreamed up in London, though like most shoes (other than Gina) manufactured in Italy, are worn by the most high-profile women in the world – Liz Hurley, Kylie Minogue, and Kate Winslet to name but a few.

And with Choo shoes we have something new in the mix – for once women making shoes for women. The

right *Jennifer Lopez arriving on the red carpet for the 2001 Golden Globe Awards in Beverly Hills. Her outfit combines diamonds, satin, and silver stilettos, successfully creating an image of pampered luxury, glamour, and success.*

overleaf *High-fashion stilettos strut the catwalk, from left to right: thigh-length, stiletto-heeled boots in rose print by Paul Costelloe in 2003; a pair in dramatic black for Givenchy's Spring/Summer 2003 collection; and a citrus-yellow and green-yellow stiletto in the Spring/Summer 2002 Versace couture collection.*

key practitioners of stiletto design have always been men – Ferragamo, Jourdan, Pfister, Vivier, Louboutin, an interesting paradox as they are least likely to wear them outside the drag act or fancy-dress party. For Sandra Choi and Tamara Mellon, the shoes have to be wearable; thus Choi won't design above a 4in [10cm] heel without adding a small platform to compensate for the angle of the foot and add balance, "Don't let the shoes wear you, wear the shoes." [xvii] As Choi sees it,

"the Choo heel is not a killer heel … When women think Jimmy Choo they think diamanté … evening … sexy shoe. The shoes are accessible, people can browse and afford, it's not an intimidating brand." [xviii]

Those who are prepared to wear Choo shoes are increasing, and what has really catapulted the brand into a more global awareness is the very public hook-up with the Oscars ceremony in Hollywood. Here Choo set up shop first at L'Hermitage and then the Peninsula Hotel in Beverly Hills for a week prior to the awards to cater for stars who decide to change their outfit at the last moment and subsequently need matching shoes. As a dress has the potential to make or break a career – think Liz Hurley in Versace in 1994 – exasperated stylists can now breathe a sigh of relief as Choo provides 20 different styles of shoe, which are then coloured and beaded to match the designer gowns. At the 2002 Oscars, "we had to make three pairs of shoes for Jennifer Lopez the night before the ceremony, because she couldn't decide which outfit to wear," [xix] recalls Mellon, while Julianne Moore decided to change her gown only three hours before the ceremony, so stepped on to the red carpet with her Choos still wet with dye. Three of the most recent Oscar winners – Julia Roberts, Hilary Swank, and Halle Berry – collected their statuettes in Choos. As a result of the attendant publicity, 65 percent of Choo's shoes are now sold in the States – good for a brand with no signature style.

Jimmy Choo was the first shoe designer to be cited in *Sex and the City*. At one point Sarah Jessica Parker as Carrie bemoans her lost "Choo Choos," but seminal stylist Patricia Fielding's real allegiance was to Manolo

below *Sarah Jessica Parker as Carrie Bradshaw in* Sex and the City. *Characteristically, she is wearing her ubiquitous Manolo Blahnik heels.*

Blahnik, whose shoes have dominated the show so much that the celebrated mugging episode was screened at the 2003 exhibition of Blahnik's work at London's Design Museum. Nobody really knows just exactly when the word "Manolos" entered the English language, but it was probably Wintour's doing at American *Vogue* in the 1980s. Manolo Blahnik was first discovered in 1970 by another famed fashion editor of American *Vogue*, Diana Vreeland (1906–89), and went on to create shoes for the catwalk collection of flamboyant designer Ossie Clark (1942–96) in 1971 out of his first shop, Zapata, which had green Astroturf on the floor and fake plastic flowers. His now infamous designs were

"green suede open-toed sandals with fake cherries hanging from ribbons and ties lacing up to the knees. The second were fashioned out of electric-blue suede, hand-stitched by Manolo himself. Unfortunately he forgot to put in the pins that would support the 7in (17.5cm) rubber heels, so as the models stepped out on to Ossie's catwalk, they wobbled and buckled." [xx]

Blahnik has become a household name in the twenty-first century with his trademark sexy styles incorporating the infamous "toe cleavage," a term used for years in the shoe industry but which first came to a more public light in an article in the *Wall Street Journal* in 1984. Shoes were being read in sexual terms, so the exposé went (not for the first time!), and the article ran with the headline, "Low-Cut Trend in Women's Shoes is Exposing Toes to New Scrutiny." The American journalist wrote,

"The classic, closed-toe pump has developed a low-cut look in the so-called throat line, which means the shoe shows more of the cracks between the toes. The industry calls this 'cleavage,' and many observers find this a sexy kind of look." [xxi]

In the 1980s, toe cleavage was seen as incompatible with the look of the deadpan businesswoman – Susan Bixler, author of *The Professional Image*, said, "You have a nice suit, you're all put together, and then you look down and all of a sudden the feet are just screaming sex!" [xxii]

below *Manolo Blahnik's contribution to fashion culture was recognized in 2002 with a retrospective exhibition at the Design Museum in London. His shoe designs were displayed alongside the imagery that inspired them, including architecture, fine art, and film.*

below *Clockwise from top: Anturia, Summer 2003, a three-tone suede "leaf" shoe; Brancusi, Summer 1996 in perspex, with an aluminium heel; and Calvo, Winter 1997/1998.*

overleaf *Soya, Winter 1997/1998 by Manolo Blahnik, whose witty and evocative shoe illustrations are the first step in the long design process. Here, a glamorous red mule is held up by the slenderest of needle heels.*

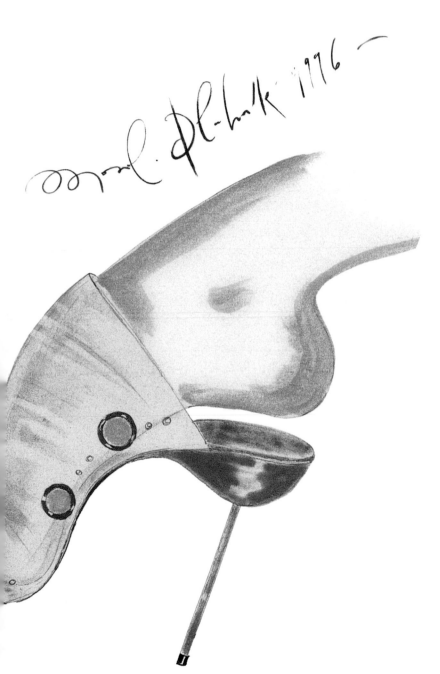

Now, however, toe cleavage is all the rage and many designers, especially Blahnik and Christian Louboutin, incorporate it into their ranges. Louboutin describes an occasion when one customer

"tried on a stiletto with low, low cleavage. She said 'I just can't have it. I show too much of my foot!' She realized she was showing without showing and suggesting something that was totally sexual. This is the difference with my shoes, the difference between *erotisme* and nudity." xxiii

Blahnik, who once said he prefers to be celibate so he can pour all of his creative juices into his work, says, "I'm no psychoanalyst, but I always knew there was an element of desire in shoes." xxiv

Blahnik describes his shoes as "more than feminine. They're sensuous. I love fairytale footwear." xxv His extravagant designs have appeared on the red carpet on the feet of Renée Zellweger and Sharon Stone, and have also have had their own supporting roles in the film *Moulin Rouge* (2002) starring Nicole Kidman. Even Madonna has extolled the delights of Blahnik's handmade stilettos, describing them as "wonderful – they last longer than sex." xxvi Blahnik sees his work as jewellery for the foot, fusing heel and toe shapes into contemporary objects of desire using influences as diverse as the Belle Epoque, bondage, and Velázquez. His eclectic design sensibility and use of materials such as Perspex, mother of pearl, and coral provide a perfect balance of aerodynamics, aesthetics, and engineering in the *haute couture* tradition of Roger Vivier and André Perugia. As Colin McDowell stresses,

"there are high-profile women … who swear they would rather die than forgo their pick of Blahnik's new styles each season. When he does his promotional show across America, many customers buy two pairs of the same style, at an average cost of six hundred US dollars [three hundred and fifty pounds] a pair, one to wear and the other for him to autograph. At one venue … sales reached almost two million US dollars [over one million pounds] in two hours." xxvii

opposite Gisele Bundchen models a pair of stiletto heels from 2002 by the Italian design duo Dolce & Gabbana. Their designs play with a voluptuous femininity as found in Italian film stars of the 1950s and '60s.

below (top) *This Carmen Miranda shoe by Terry de Havilland was designed for the film* Harry Potter and the Philosopher's Stone *(2001).*

below (bottom) *Sugar Plum Leyla, from the Glitter and Twisted range (2003) by Terry de Havilland, was named after one of de Havilland's cats; the extravagant, tasselled design has proved popular with pole dancers!*

Many women are being converted to the joys of the stiletto as a result of all this media exposure, and why not? A pair of shoes gives instant gratification no matter what body shape you are (unlike other forms of high fashion) and they alter the body without the side effects of Botox or liposuction. And as the president of Manolo Blahnik, George Malkemus, says, "they are ageless. You can be in your sixties and still look fabulous in a stiletto." [xxviii] Supermodel Veronica Webb believes that "high heels put your ass on a pedestal – where it belongs," [xxix] and the contemporary stiletto retains its erotic power and high fashion appeal. Fashionistas in London, Paris, Milan, and New York snap up the work of Johnny Moke, Gucci – known as "push-up bras for the feet" – Prada, Sergio Rossi, Cesare Paciotti, and Stephane Kelian. They may not all be able to afford a suit by Tom Ford, but they can stump up the cash for a pair of his steel-heeled stilettos, which sell out almost immediately every season. The most beautiful one-off stilettos can be sourced from the studio of master craftsman Terry de Havilland who works out of a room in the East End of London, dreaming up the most miraculous shoes on the planet for catwalk shows such as Frost-French. His work is a key inspiration for contemporary labels Miu Miu, Prada, and Dolce & Gabbana and shows British craftsmanship at its best. He designs, cuts, stitches, and hand-lasts himself, creating shoes in suede, organza, satin, and his signature snakeskin for films and for celebrities such as Jade Jagger (who has taken over from her mother Bianca as one of de Havilland's customers); and local lapdancers have been known to buy a pair or two. One style, the Sugar Plum Leyla, has a cheeky tassel hanging from the back. His wife and business partner Liz de Havilland says, "The girls ring up and say 'I've got to have some more tassels.' Once they've shred their tassels, you know they've had a good night out." [xxx]

Star status is also conferred by Gina, who name their designs after favoured clients such as Victoria Beckham and Kylie Minogue, and women wanting the alchemy of contemporary celebrity buy the style hoping some of the magic will wear off. Most women wear stilettos now, as Manolo Blahnik put it recently:

DOLCE & GABBANA

previous page *Giuseppe Pacinti established Cesare Pacintti in 1948 as a company specialising in men's classic shoes. In the 1990s, his son and daughter, Cesare and Paolo, developed a women's range that has become associated with high-fashion, high-rise stilettos.*

right *Gina Shoes is the last British company to be both designing and manufacturing shoes in London. Their craft skills have been handed down through each generation of the family. Its client list includes Madonna, Whitney Houston, Nicole Kidman, and Jade Jagger.*

"Women who love high heels used to be like a tribe. There were women who wore high heels all of the time, and then there were other women who always wore flats. Now that line is being crossed. Many women wear tiny heels during the day, and then for evenings or glamorous occasions, they wear very high heels." xxxi

Not all women can walk in high heels, though, as it requires stamina, determination, and training. One trainer in London, Marco Bellagamba (literally "beautiful leg"), realized that many of his clients were having problems, complaining of puffed-out feet and swollen ankles, so devised a special series of exercises for women who were having problems staying upright on their Manolos for longer than a few minutes. His high-heel workout concentrates on strengthening the ankles to prevent equinus, a tightening of the calves common among novice stiletto wearers. Bellagamba advises women to limit their heel-wearing to less than five hours. Many designers tend to stress that their shoes are comfortable and the director of public relations at Jimmy Choo, Tara Ffrench Mullen, prides herself on cycling to work every day in a pair of Choo stilettos. Christian Louboutin, designer of the highest, most subversive, and witty heels in fashion is more sanguine:

"The stiletto is a feminine weapon that men don't have, but women come into the shop and they complain. They say 'I can't walk, I can't run in these shoes!' I say 'Why run? In the reality of life, nobody's running.... If you walk in a certain rhythm you can watch the city, see the buildings, you see more of the landscape—and it permits men to stop you – otherwise you cross life without seeing it." xxxii

Louboutin sees the impracticality of the stiletto as an opportunity for an erotic encounter – he is perhaps the only shoe designer working in the twenty-first century who truly understands the legacy and sexual power of the stiletto. He is almost the embodiment of the supreme shoe designer of Geoff Nicholson's *Footsucker* (1995) who designs the most beautiful yet subversive and dangerous shoes. One pair by Louboutin had heels that were

opposite *Christian Louboutin, the supreme stiletto designer of the twenty-first century, creates shoes "for women trying to reach the sky." He believes that a shoe on a woman is an extension of herself.*

below *The Troulala stiletto (*Winter *2003–4) by Louboutin goes beyond the subtle sexual suggestion of toe cleavage. In his words, "the toe – it's peeking out just waiting to be kissed!"*

"long and slender, tapering almost to a point, and made of … burnished red metal. The shoes had peep-toes, the opening more or less semi-circular, the edge of that opening and the edge of the shoe's mouth, again braided with the same red metal. The body of the shoe was made out of some supremely soft inky black leather, but a tracery of thin red-metal filaments ran across it, less regular than a spider's web, more like spilled wax." xxxiii

The novel describes how shoes have the power to mesmerize , and that only a few can respond to the power of the stiletto as fetish in a truly sexual sense. Louboutin's shoes are such shoes, experimental in design and frankly erotic in their final execution. As he states bluntly, "The last thing I would like is for people to point to my shoes and say, 'Oh, they look so comfortable.'" xxxiv Originally apprenticed to Charles Jourdan, Louboutin opened his own atelier in 1991. He has always been obsessed with heels, and recalls being in the Lunar Park in Paris around the age of ten and seeing

"a woman, quite shabby, all in black, big hair like Kim Novak. She was wearing a black *tailleur* and black stockings with a seam up the back. She had spiky heels – I could not believe it! I followed her, I was really following her shoes for half an hour. At one point a guy grabbed me by the shoulder, kicked my arse and said 'You! Move!' I was following a prostitute." xxxv

Louboutin's fascination with her stilettos was due to their practical non-appearance on the streets of Paris in the 1970s, when the wedge and chunky heel were dominating footwear fashions. He had never seen stiletto heels, only a diagrammatic drawing of a pair on a sign in the Musée Oceanographique, forbidding the wearing of spindle heels in the museum because they had been destroying the mosaic floors in the 1960s. That sign fired his imagination, for he

"could not believe someone could design something so curious and I realized that I could draw something that did not exist. I realized you could do what you want with a drawing of a shoe. Little by little I collected information and people began to bring

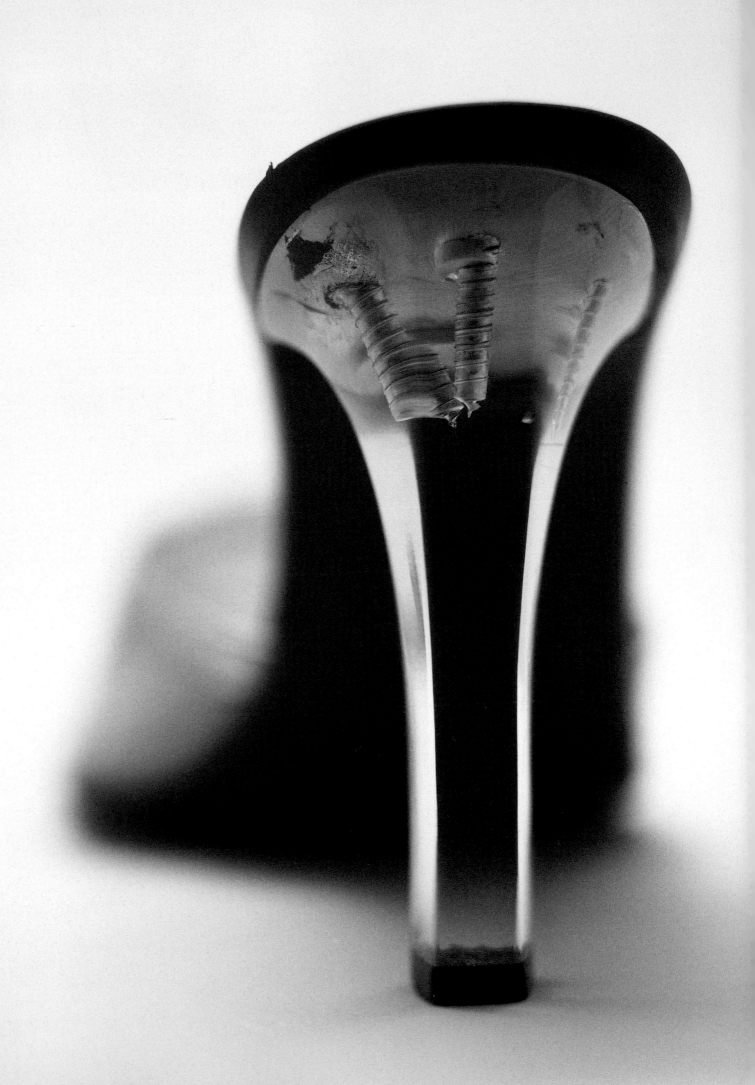

previous page *A series of stiletto shoes by Christian Louboutin for Summer 2003. Clockwise from top left: Kobe, a slingback shoe using a surrealist male tie as front detail; Mignonette, in bronze with ankle strap; Just-Nothing, with a transparent front that makes the sole appear self-supporting; and Cyclopette, designed to display sexy toe cleavage.*

left *The Perspex heel of this prototype Trash Mule by Christian Louboutin gives an insight into the shoe's construction by laying bare the screw tips used to anchor the heel to the shoe.*

anything about shoes to school for me. Someone gave me a gold book, nothing on the cover, just the name Roger Vivier and I saw these incredible shoes … My God! It can really be a job!" xxxvi

At the age of 17 Louboutin began to visit backstage at Les Folies Bergère and the Lido, sketching and observing the showgirls, "partly for the enjoyment of the performance, the glitter and sequins, but mostly to watch the way they walked," xxxvii and he became somewhat of a "mascot at the place." xxxviii He realized that the relationship between the dancer and her shoes was of the utmost importance: she had to descend long stairs, parade, jump, and do the splits while wearing a towering headdress and heels that were almost as extreme as the *en pointe* of ballet. He saw that the balance between shoe and heel was paramount, as the dancer could never look down at her feet to find her way or she would destroy the illusion of control and grace. The high heels were also being worn by the most sexy and glamorous women he had ever seen. These formative years translate into striking silhouettes, towering heels, and designs that have an erotic tension, be it the exhibition of toe cleavage in the shoe Troulala where the exposed toe is almost absurdly sexualized and ripe for ravishment, or his gladiator boots worn by many female stars who like the "glamazon" feeling – part stripper, part warrior – that they evoke. As Louboutin says of his perfect customer, "she may die, but she'll die in high heels. That way there'll always be a spark of life." xxxix

For many women, then, the new stiletto encompasses many different viewpoints. For some it is a shoe of immense sexual power, a literally walking embodiment of post-feminist power; for others a symbol of their status and bankability with the designer tag being its most important aspect. As ever it's glamour over comfort, and sex rather than succour. For they are still a torture to wear, exaggerating the arch of the foot and, according to the many detractors in the mass media, the cause of a virtual epidemic of lower back pain. Vertiginous heels can also adversely affect the subtaler joint, just below the ankle, and the Achilles' tendon.

below *The Cecile by Anya Hindmarch, 2004. Hindmarch has been a highly successful accessories designer since 1993, particularly famed for her luxury leather bags. In 2002, she entered the lucrative shoe market with her first range, incorporating the perennially popular stiletto.*

As Carmen Borgonovo wrote in *W* magazine in 2002,

"In addition, if the pitch of the heel is too high, the body's weight is redistributed to the ball of the foot, which can cause or aggravate bunions, hammer toes, corns, and inflammatory nerve conditions." [xl]

After 15 or 20 years of wearing a particular heel silhouette, your foot starts taking the form of your shoe," says Steven Weinfeld MD, assistant professor of orthopaedic surgery at Mount Sinai Medical Center in New York. President of Manolo Blahnik, George Malkemus attests "When my Park Avenue clients in their seventies and eighties take off their designer shoes, their feet look exactly like their shoes." [xli]

Women, however, are prepared to take the pain to gain the allure of the stiletto. Journalist Ann Magnuson admitted just such a trade-off in 1994, describing how,

"the bones in my ankle cracked and my Achilles' tendons bent backward …. My ass felt bigger than a Buick, and my thighs … swung back and forth like a couple of sides of beef. Are these shoes disempowering? … Are we rendered helpless by wearing them? The answer is Yes! Yes! Of course! What other point would there be in wearing them?" [xlii]

As original stiletto wearers in the 1950s were alleged to have amputated their little toes for the perfect fit, so reports surfaced in 2003 of a new, extreme solution to which women were resorting – surgery. One stiletto obsessive reportedly spent more than five thousand pounds (ten thousand US dollars) on an operation to cure the bunions she had developed through wearing Blahniks and Choos, "My feet ached so much I was having to wear flip-flops instead of dressing up and going out." [xliii] The American surgeon

"shortened her second toe by removing a piece of bone, straightened her little toe, and cut off a bunion. Her operation took place in February, so she could enjoy the summer in peek-a-boo sandals." [xliv]

below *Backstage at a Fusha Show for New York Fashion Week, Winter 2003. A model ties a white leather ankle boot with winklepicker toe and stiletto heel, a style worn by celebrities such as Beyoncé, Jennifer Lopez, and Britney Spears in 2004.*

opposite *Under the design direction of Tom Ford, Gucci began producing metal-heeled stilettos in the mid-1990s. The implicit threat of the design in this pair, dating from 2000, is reinforced by the subtly fetishistic leg ties.*

When Blahnik announced that in 2003 his shoes would be 20 percent narrower and pointed, it appeared the cult of the tiny foot was still among us, so a bit of foot trimming seems to be in order. Dr Suzanne Levine is the most widely recognized "foot-facelift doctor," and describes clients in their forties and fifties who "still want to look good" saying, "I'm not going to give up my high heels." [xlv] Even Sarah Jessica Parker confesses, "I've destroyed my feet completely, but I don't care. What do you really need your feet for anyway?" [xlvi]

The stiletto lives on, as it has for most of the twentieth century. Contemporary designers are responding again to the elegant modernity of the heel, pushing it to the limits of height, slimness, and wearability. But boundaries can be pushed too far. According to one journalist, Manolo Blahnik was

"once forced to pull a pair of razor-sharp 3½in [9cm] titanium-heeled stilettos from production because his 'killer heels' were too dangerous. Indeed, the heels – which were as thin as the ink tube in a ballpoint – could effortlessly cut through carpet and, more worryingly, human flesh and bone. Blahnik was also made aware that these shoes could easily be mistaken for weapons when luggage was x-rayed at airports." [xlvii]

The sleek silhouette of the stiletto makes it a uniquely modern shoe in the midst of fashion, which operates in the main around a "fake historicism," [xlviii] as fashion writer Colin McDowell puts it. It can be an object of pure sexuality in the hands of Christian Louboutin, a piece of feminine frippery to lust after by Jimmy Choo, or an object akin to sculpture by Blahnik. It can even embody the animal-rights ethics of Stella McCartney, whose vegetarian stilettos remove eco-fashion from the worthy to the downright sexy.

Since the stiletto's inception in the 1950s, its chameleon-like quality has made it a powerful symbol. Moving from fetish to high fashion and back again, it has always kept that hint of danger. In the battle of the sexes the stiletto (but maybe not the wearer) will always be on top.

GUCCI

FOOTNOTES

See bibliography on page 173 for full details of works by cited authors.

Introduction

i   William A. Rossi, p.131.
ii   Mary Trasko, p.65.
iii   Margaret Visser, p.37.
iv   Richard von Kraft-Ebbing, p.14.
v   Quentin Bell, p.37.
vi   Colin McDowell, p.121.
vii   Marcel Danesi, preface.
viii   Shoshana Goldberg, "Killer Heels," in *Shoo Magazine*, Summer 2003, p.46.
ix   Rita Freedman, p.76.
x   *Eadem*, p.78.
xi   Margaret Visser, p.124.
xii   www.artphoto.u-net.com/shoebox

Fancy Footwork

i   Catalogue to exhibition, *Salvatore Ferragamo: The Art of the Shoe 1927–1960* (London, Victoria and Albert Museum, 1988) p.27.
ii   Diana Vreeland, p.40.
iii   Ann Scott-James, p.121.
iv   *Footwear* magazine, 1948.
v   Penny Sparke, *As Long as It's Pink*, p.166.
vi   Coventry Patmore.
vii   Veronica Dengel, p.8.
viii   Sue Townsend, "Gone To Seed," in *The Sunday Times Style* magazine, 11 May 2003.
ix   Pearson Philips, p.134.
x   *Harper's Bazaar* UK, October 1945.
xi   Lou Taylor, "Paris Couture 1940–1944," *Chic Thrills: A Fashion Reader*, ed. Juliet Ash and Elizabeth Wilson (London, Pandora Press, 1992) p.138.
xii   Pearson Philips, p.134.
xiii   *Ibid.*
xiv   *Idem*, p.144.
xv   *Footwear* magazine, February 1947.
xvi   Mrs Robert Henrey, p.139.
xvii   *Ibid.*
xviii   Colombe Pringle, p.11.
xix   *Ibid.*
xx   *Vogue* USA, March 1954.
xxi   *Vogue* USA, July 1953.
xxii   Hermina Black, p.5.
xxiii   Mary Trasko, p.85.
xxiv   Linda O'Keefe, p.409.
xxv   Barbara Cox, interview with author, June 2003.
xxvi   *Ibid.*
xxvii   Ginette Spanier, p.182.
xxviii   *Ibid.*
xxix   Penny Sparke, *As Long as It's Pink*, p.182.
xxx   Lesley Jackson, p.42.
xxxi   Thomas Hine, p.112.
xxxii   *Vogue* UK, April 1950, p.81.
xxxiii   Barbara Cox, interview with author, June 2003.
xxxiv   *Ibid.*
xxxv   Veronica Dengel, p.31.
xxxvi   Pearson Philips, p.137.
xxxvii   Eileen Allen, p.26.
xxxviii   Ethelind Fearon, p.59.
xxxix   *Ibid.*
xl   Betty Page, p.23.
xli   Eileen McCarthy, p.83.
xlii   "The Hazards of the Stiletto Heel," in *Picture Post*, 19 December 1953.
xliii   *Ibid.*
xliv   Mehmet Kurdash, interview with author, June 2003.
xlv   *The Times*, 3 June 1957.
xlvi   *Ibid.*

Hollywood Heels

i   Eileen Allen, p.153.
ii   Salvatore Ferragamo, *Shoemaker of Dreams*.
iii   Salvatore Ferragamo, *The Art of the Shoe*, p.27.
iv   *Ibid.*
v   Idem *The Art of the Shoe*, p.35.
vi   Lee Wright, p.11.
vii   Colin McDowell, *Shoes: Fashion and Fantasy*, p.47.
viii   Mehmet Kurdash, interview with author, June 2003.
ix   Stephen Bayley, Philippe Garner and Deyan Sudjic, p.176.
x   Barbara Cox, interview with author, May 2003.
xi   Ken Cox, interview with author, May 2003.
xii   Toni del Renzio, "Shoes, Hair, and Coffee in Ark Twenty," *Journal of the Royal College of Art*, *c*.1957.

xiii   Len Deighton in Dick Hebdige, p.75.
xiv   Colin MacInnes, p.32.
xv   *Idem*, pp.17–18.
xvi   *Idem*, pp.62–3.
xvii   *Ibid.*
xviii   www.womenshistory.about.com/cs/quotes/
xix   Maurice Zolotow, p.70.
xx   *Idem*, p.127.
xxi   Anthony Summers p.44.
xxii   www.fashion-planet.com
xxiii   www.womenshistory.about.com/cs/quotes/
xxiv   Lynne Reid Banks, p.101.
xxv   Betty Page, p.184.
xxvi   Ken Cox, interview with author, May 2003.
xxvii   Stan Barstow, p.33.
xxviii   *Idem*, p.215.
xxix   John Braine, *Room at the Top* in Judith Watt, p.154.
xxx   Mehmet Kurdash, interview with author, June 2003.
xxxi   Barbara Cox, interview with author, May 2003.
xxxii   Ken Cox, interview with author, June 2003.
xxxiii   Charles Hamblett and Jane Deverson, p.94.
xxxiv   Lynne Reid Banks, p.114.
xxxv   Barbara Cox, interview with author, May 2003.
xxxvi   Eileen Melinkoff, p.45.
xxxvii   Florence E. Ledger, p.11.
xxxviii   Eileen Melinkoff, p.87.
xxxix   George M.D. Bankoff, pp.93–4.
xl   Harry Roberts, p.266.
xli   *Ibid.*
xlii   Mary Trasko, p.71.
xliii   David Kunzle.
xliv   *Idem*, p.278.
xlv   Mary Davis Peters, p.45.
xlvi   Eileen Allen, pp.142–3.
xlvii   Florence E. Ledger, p.171.
xlviii   *Idem*, p.278.
xlix   *Idem*, p.279.
l   *Shoe and Leather News*, 3 July 1958.
li   "UK Firm Designs Disc Heel as Alternative to Stiletto Type," in *Footwear News*, 20 December 1962.

Spikes and Lashes

i   Cecil Willet-Cunningham in David Kunzle, pp.19–20.
ii   Sigmund Freud.
iii   Rétif de la Bretonne in Hans-Jurgen Dopp, p.41.
iv   Gilles Deleuze, *Masochism* (New York, Zone Books, 1991) p.31.
v   Sigmund Freud, p.354.
vi   *Ibid.*
vii   Richard von Kraft-Ebbing, p.70.
viii   *Ibid.*
ix   Geoff Nicholson, p.34.
x   *Idem*, p.154
xi   Leopold von Sacher-Masoch, p.47.
xii   Hans Christian Andersen, pp.47–8.
xiii   *Ibid.*
xiv   leather@netins.net, *The Stiletto Trap* (2003).
xv   *Ibid.*
xvi   Bruno Bettelheim, p.265.
xvii   *Ibid.*
xviii   *Idem*, p.64
xix   Morgana Baron, p.95.
xx   Paula Sanchez, in www.geocities.com
xxi   David Kunzle, p.19.
xxii   *Idem*, supplementary material.
xxiii   William A. Rossi, pp.119–20.
xxiv   Simone de Beauvoir, p.543.
xxv   Joan Cassell, pp.82–3.
xxvi   Marilyn French, p.74.
xxvii   Germaine Greer, p.31.
xxviii   Karen Durbin in Angela Neustatter, p.92.
xxix   Susan Brownmiller, p.143.
xxx   Jean Rook in Tamasin Doe, p.42.
xxxi   Terry de Havilland, interview with author, August 2003.
xxxii   *Ibid.*
xxxiii   *Ibid.*
xxxiv   *Ibid.*
xxxv   *Ibid.*
xxxvi   *Ibid.*
xxxvii   *Ibid.*
xxxviii   Peter York, *Style Wars* (London, Sidgwick and Jackson, 1980) p.136.
xxxix   Vivienne Westwood in Caroline Evans and Minna Thornton, p.24.
xl   Ted Polhemus, "Punk 1977," in *Vogue* UK, December 1977.
xli   John T. Molloy, p.34.

xlii   *Idem*, p.66.
xliii   *Idem*, p.78.
xliv   Charlotte du Cann, "Thatcherstyle," *New Statesman and Society*, October 1989, p.48.
xlv   Shirley Conran, p.452.
xlvi   Jilly Cooper, p.409.
xlvii   Anne Billson, pp.171–2.
xlviii   *Ibid.*
xlix   *Ibid.*
l   *Eadem*, p.207.
li   Eileen McCauley, *The Seduction: A Clumsy Poem of Teenage Angst* (© Bennet Warburton, *c*.1980s).
lii   Peter York p.57.

Balancing Act

i   Maggie Alderson, pp.73–4.
ii   *George* magazine (Washington D.C., USA), August 2000.
iii   *Sex in the City*, HBO Television, USA.
iv   Shelagh Young in Lorraine Gamman and Margaret Marchment, p.178.
v   Gill Hudson in *The Guardian*, 30 January 1990, p.20.
vi   Judith Lewis, "Reconsidering the Stiletto," in *Los Angeles Weekly*, 23 July 2000.
vii   *Ibid.*
viii   *Ibid.*
ix   *Ibid.*
x   André Leon Talley in Justine Picardie, "The Man Who Makes the Sexiest Shoes in the World," in *Vogue* UK, February 2003.
xi   Toby Young, pp.67–8.
xii   Tamsin Blanchard, pp. 76–7.
xiii   Carmen Navarro Pedrosa, p.220.
xiv   Claudia Croft, "Heel the World," in *The Sunday Times Style* magazine, 19 January 2003, p.4.
xv   Claudia Croft, "Heel the World," p.5.
xvi   *Ibid.*
xvii   Sandra Choi, interview with author, August 2003.
xviii   *Ibid.*
xix   Claudia Croft, "Heel the World," p.4.
xx   Justine Picardie, "The Man Who Makes the Sexiest Shoes in the World," *Vogue* UK, February 2003, p.190.
xxi   *Wall Street Journal*, 1984.
xxii   Susan Bixler.
xxiii   Christian Louboutin, interview with author, July 2003.
xxiv   Justine Picardie, "The Man Who Makes the Sexiest Shoes in the World," *Vogue* UK, February 2003, p.190.
xxv   *Ibid.*
xxvi   Shoshana Goldberg, "Killer Heels," in *Shoo Magazine*, Summer 2003, p.46.
xxvii   Colin McDowell, "Manolo," in *The Sunday Times Style* magazine, 19 January 2003.
xxviii   George Malkemus, "High and Mighty," by Carmen Borgonovo in *W* magazine, September 2002, p.374.
xxix   Nancy Etcoff, p.195.
xxx   Liz de Havilland, interview with author, August 2003.
xxxi   Interview, *Night Moves*, BBC Radio 4, 31 January 2003.
xxxii   Christian Louboutin, interview with author, July 2003.
xxxiii   Geoff Nicholson, p.67.
xxxiv   Christian Louboutin, interview with author, July 2003.
xxxv   *Ibid.*
xxxvi   *Ibid.*
xxxvii   *Ibid.*
xxxviii   *Ibid.*
xxxix   *Ibid.*
xl   Carmen Borgonovo, "High and Mighty,".
xli   George Malkemus "High and Mighty," p.376.
xlii   Ann Magnuson, "Hell on Heels," in *Allure*, September 1994.
xliii   Sarah Baxter, "Fashion Victims Have Their Toes Trimmed to Fit Shoes," in *The Sunday Times*, 31 August 2003.
xliv   *Ibid.*
xlv   *Ibid.*
xlvi   Sarah Jessica Parker in Shoshana Goldberg, "Killer Heels," in *Shoo Magazine*, Summer 2003, p.47.
xlvii   Shoshana Goldberg, "Killer Heels," p.46.
xlviii   Colin McDowell.

BIBLIOGRAPHY

Alderson, Maggie. *Shoe Money*, London, Penguin, 1980
Allen, Eileen. *The Book of Beauty*, London, George Newnes Ltd, 1961
Andersen, Hans Christian. *Fairy Tales and Legends*, London, Bodley Head, 1935
Ash, Juliet and Elizabeth Wilson (eds.). *Chic Thrills: A Fashion Reader*, London, Pandora Press, 1992
Bankoff, George MD. *The Essential Eve: A Guide to Women's Perfection*, London, Cassell, 1952
Baron, Morgana. *Rue Marquis de Sade*, London, Nexus, 1996
Barstow, Stan. *A Kind of Loving*, London, Penguin, 1960
Baudot, François. *Salvatore Ferragamo*, New York, Universe Publishing, 2000
Bayley, Stephen. *In Good Shape*, London, The Design Council, 1979
Bayley, Stephen, Philippe Garner, and Deyan Sudjic, *Twentieth Century Style and Design*, London, Thames and Hudson, 1986
Baynes, Ken and Kate. *The Shoe Show: British Shoes since 1790*, London, Crafts Council, 1979
Beauvoir, Simone de. *The Second Sex*, London, Penguin, 1972
Bell, Quentin. *On Human Finery*, London, Allison and Busby, 1992
Bettelheim, Bruno. *The Uses of Enchantment: The Meaning and Importance of Fairy Tales*, New York, Alfred Knopf, 1976
Billson, Anne. *Suckers: Bleeding London Dry*, London, Pan Books, 1993
Bixler, Susan. *The Professional Image*, New York, Putnam, 1984
Black, Hermina. *In Pursuit of Perilla*, London, Hodder and Stoughton, 1958
Blanchard, Tamsin. *The Shoe: Best Foot Forward*, London, Carlton Books, 2000
Bond, David. *Glamour in Fashion*, Enfield, Guinness Publishers, 1992
Braine, John. *Room at the Top*, (1957) London, Arrow, 1989
Brownmiller, Susan. *Femininity*, London, Grafton Books, 1984
Bruzzi, Stella. *Undressing Cinema: Clothes, Identities, Films*, London, Routledge, 1997
Burchill, Julie and Tony Parsons. *The Boy Looked at Johnny: The Obituary of Rock and Roll*, London, Pluto Press, 1978
Carter, Angela. *The Sadeian Woman*, London, Virago, 1979
Eadem, *Nothing Sacred: Selected Writings*, London, Virago, 1982
Cassell, Joan. *A Group Called Women: Sisterhood and Symbolism in the Feminist Movement*, New York, David McKay, 1977
Castle, Philip. *Airshow*, London, Dragon's World, 1989
Catalogue to Exhibition, *Salvatore Ferragamo: The Art of the Shoe*, London, Victoria and Albert Museum, 1988
Catalogue to Exhibition, *Salvatore Ferragamo*, Florence, Centro Di della Edifimi srl, 1987
Clifford, Patrick. *The Green Stiletto*, Dublin, Mellifont Press, 1939
Coleridge, Nicholas. *The Fashion Conspiracy: The Dazzling Inside Story of the Glamorous World of International High Fashion*, New York, Harper and Row, 1988
Conran, Shirley. *Lace*, London, Penguin, 1982
Cooper, Jilly. *Rivals*, London, Corgi, 1989
Craik, Jennifer. *The Face of Fashion: Cultural Studies in Fashion*, London, Routledge, 1994
Danesi, Marcel. *Cigarettes, High Heels and Other Interesting Things: An Introduction to Semiotics*, London, Macmillan Press, 1999
Davis Peters, Mary. *Modern Living: Your Looks*, London, Longmans, 1963
Dengel, Veronica. *Can I Hold My Beauty*, London, John Westhouse Publishers, 1946
Dior, Christian. *Dior by Dior*, London, Penguin, 1957
Doe, Tamasin. *Patrick Cox: Wit, Irony, and Footwear*, London, Thames and Hudson, 1998
Dopp, Hans-Jurgen. *Feet-ishism*, New York, Parkstone Press Ltd, 2001

Dyer, Richard. *Stars*, London, BFI Publishing, 1988
Edwards, Janet Radcliffe. *The Sceptical Feminist*, London, Routledge and Kegan Paul, 1980
Etcoff, Nancy. *Survival of the Prettiest: The Science of Beauty*, New York, Doubleday, 1999
Evans, Caroline and Minna Thornton. *Women and Fashion: A New Look*, London, Quartet Books, 1989
Fearon, Ethelind. *How to Keep Pace with Your Daughter*, London, Herbert Jenkins Ltd, 1958
Ferragamo, Salvatore. *Shoemaker of Dreams: The Autobiography of Salvatore Ferragamo*, Giunti Gruppo Editoriale, 1985
Ferragamo, Salvatore et al. *The Art of the Shoe 1898–1960*, New York, Rizzoli, 1993
Flugel, J.C. *The Psychology of Clothing* (1930), New York, International Universities Press, Inc., 1971
Fogg, Marnie. *Boutique*, London, Mitchell Beazley, 2003
Freedman, Rita. *Beauty Bound: Why Women Strive for Physical Perfection*, London, Columbus Books, 1988
French, Marilyn. *The Bleeding Heart*, London, André Deutsch, 1980
Friedan, Betty. *The Feminine Mystique*, Harmondsworth, Penguin, 1976
Freud, Sigmund. *On Sexuality*, London, Penguin, 1977
Gamman, Lorraine and Margaret Marshment (eds.). *The Female Gaze: Women as Viewers of Popular Culture*, London, The Women's Press, 1988
Gamman, Lorraine and Merja Makinen. *Female Fetishism: A New Look*, London, Lawrence and Wishart, 1994
Goodwin, Ernest. *Stiletto*, W. Collins Sons and Co. Ltd, 1924
Greer, Germaine. *The Female Eunuch*, London, Paladin, 1971
Hamblett, Charles and Jane Deverson. *Generation X*, London, Tandem Books Ltd, 1964
Hebdige, Dick. *Subculture: The Meaning of Style*, London, Methuen, 1979
Idem. *Hiding in the Light: On Images and Things*, London, Routledge, 1988
Henrey, Mrs Robert. *This Feminine World*, London, J.M. Dent and Sons, 1956
Hine, Thomas. *Populuxe*, London, Bloomsbury, 1987
Jackson, Lesley. *The New Look: Design in the 1950s*, London, Thames and Hudson, 1991
Kirkham, Pat (ed.). *The Gendered Object*, Manchester, Manchester University Press, 1996
König, René. *The Restless Image*, London, Allen and Unwin, 1973
Kraft-Ebbing, Richard von. *Psychopathia Sexualis*, New York, Creation Books, 1997
Kunzle, David. *Fashion and Fetishism*, New Jersey, Rowman and Littlefield, 1982
Langner, Lawrence. *The Importance of Wearing Clothes*, London, Constable and Co. Ltd, 1955
Ledger, Florence E. *Put Your Foot Down: A Treatise on the History of Shoes*, Melksham, Colin Venton, 1976
Liggitt, Arline and John. *The Tyranny of Beauty*, New York, Gollancz, 1989
MacInnes, Colin. *Absolute Beginners* (1959), London, Allison and Busby, 1980
McCarthy, Eileen. *Frankly Feminine*, London, The Grolier Society, 1965
McDowell, Colin. *Shoes: Fashion and Fantasy*, London, Thames and Hudson, 1989
Idem. *Manolo Blahnik*, London, Cassell and Co., 2000
Melinkoff, Eileen. *What We Wore: An Offbeat Social History of Women's Clothing 1950–1980*, New York, Quill, 1984
Molloy, John T. *Women: Dress for Success*, London, W. Foulsham and Co. Ltd, 1980
Neustatter, Angela. *Hyenas in Petticoats: A Look at Twenty Years of Feminism*, London, Penguin, 1989
Nicholson, Geoff. *Footsucker*, London, Victor Gollancz, 1995
O'Keefe, Linda. *Shoes: A Celebration of Pumps, Sandals, Slippers, and More*, New York, Workman Publishing Company Inc., 1996

Page, Betty. *On Fair Vanity*, London, Convoy Publications Ltd, 1954
Patmore, Coventry. *The Poems of Coventry Patmore*, introduction by Frederick Page, Oxford University Press, 1949
Pattison, Angela and Nigel Cawthorne. *A Century of Shoes: Icons of Style in the Twentieth Century*, London, Quarto, 1997
Pedrosa, Navarro Carmen. *The Rise and Fall of Imelda Marcos*, Manila, SSP Makati, 1987
Penzer, N.M. *The Harem* (1936), London, Spring Books, 1965
Philips, Pearson. Essay in Michael Sissons and Philip French (eds.). *Age of Austerity 1945–1951*, London, Penguin, 1964
Polhemus, Ted. *Bodystyles*, London, Lennard Publishing, 1988
Pratt, Lucy and Linda Woolley. *Shoes*, London, V&A Publications, 1999
Pringle, Colombe. *Roger Vivier*, London, Thames and Hudson, 1999
Probert, Christina. *Shoes in Vogue since 1910*, London, Thames and Hudson, 1981
Reid Banks, Lynne. *The L-Shaped Room*, London, Penguin, 1960
Ricci, Stefania (ed.). *Cinderella: The Shoe Rediscovered*, Milan, Musée Salvatore Ferragamo, 1998
Roberts, Harry. *The Practical Way to Keep Fit*, London, Odhams Press, c.1960
Rossi, William A. *The Sex Life of the Foot and Shoe*, London, Routledge and Kegan Paul, 1977
Sacher-Masoch, Leopold von. *Venus in Furs*, London, Luxor Press, 1965
Scott-James, Ann. *In the Mink*, London, Purnell and Sons, 1953
Spanier, Ginette. *It Isn't All Mink*, London, Collins, 1959
Sparke, Penny. *As Long as It's Pink: The Sexual Politics of Taste*, London, Pandora, 1995
Eadem, *Italian Design: 1870 to the Present*. London, Thames and Hudson, 1988
Stacey, Jackie. *Star Gazing: Hollywood Cinema and Female Spectatorship*, London, Routledge, 1994
Steele, Valerie. *Shoes: A Lexicon of Style*, London, Scriptum Editions, 1998
Eadem, *Fetish: Fashion, Sex, and Power*, Oxford, Oxford University Press, 1996
Eadem, *Fashion: Italian Style*, Yale, Yale University Press, 2003
Summers, Anthony. *Goddess: The Secret Lives of Marilyn Monroe*, London, Victor Gollancz Ltd, 1985
Tam, Viviene. *China Chic*, New York, Regam Books, 2000
Trasko, Mary. *Heavenly Soles: Extraordinary Twentieth Century Shoes*, New York, Abbeville Press, 1989
Visser, Margaret. *The Way We Are*, London, Penguin, 1997
Vreeland, Diana. *DV*, New York, Random House, 1985
Watt, Judith. *The Penguin Book of Twentieth Century Fashion Writing*, London, Penguin, 2000
White, Nicola. *Reconstructing Italian Fashion*, London, Berg, 2000
Wilson, Elizabeth. *Adorned in Dreams: Fashion and Modernity*, London, Virago, 1985
Wilson, Elizabeth and Lou Taylor. *Through the Looking Glass*, London, BBC Books, 1989
Wright, Lee. "Objectifying Gender: the Stiletto Heel," in Judy Attfield, and Pat Kirkham (eds.). *A View From the Interior: Feminism, Women, and Design*, London, Women's Press, 1989
York, Peter. *Style Wars*, London, Sidgwick and Jackson, 1980
Idem. *Peter York's The Eighties*, London, BBC Books, 1995
Young, Toby. *How to Lose Friends and Alienate People*, London, Abacus, 2002
Zolotow, Maurice. *Marilyn Monroe: An Uncensored Biography*, London, W.H. Allen and Co. 1960

DIRECTORY

Where to buy

L.K. BENNETT
London
31 Brook Street, W1Y 1AJ
+44 (0)20 7491 3005
Paris
31 rue de Grenelle
75007 Paris
+33 1 422 22080

MANOLO BLAHNIK
London
49–51 Old Church Street
SW3 5BS
+44 (0)20 7352 8622
New York
13 West 54th Street, NY 10012
+1 212 582 3007

JIMMY CHOO
London
27 New Bond Street, W1S 2RH
+44 (0)20 7493 5858
Milan
Via San Pietro All'Orto
20121 Milano
+39 2 4548 1770
New York
716 Madison Ave, NY 10021
+1 212 759 7078

SALVATORE FERRAGAMO
London
24 Old Bond Street, W1S 4AL
+44 (0)20 7629 5007
Milan
Via Montenapoleone 3
20121 Milano
+39 2 77111446
New York
661 Fifth Avenue
Trump Tower, NY 10022
+1 212 759 3822

KURT GEIGER
London
65 South Molton Street
W1K 5SU
+44 (0)20 7546 1888

GINA
London
9 Old Bond Street, W1X 3TA
+44 (0)20 7409 7090

GUCCI
London
34 Old Bond Street, W1S 4QL
+44 (0)20 7629 2716
Paris
2 rue du Faubourg St Honoré
75008 Paris
+33 1 449 41460

New York
840 Madison Ave, NY 10021
+1 212 717 2619

TERRY DE HAVILLAND
London
TDH London, Office 2
118–122 Grafton Road
NW5 4BA
Fax +44 7092 808 887

EMMA HOPE
London
33 Amwell Street, EC1R 1UR
+44 (0)20 7259 9566

CHARLES JOURDAN
Paris
86 avenue des Champs-Elysées
75008 Paris
+33 1 456 22928
New York
777 Madison Ave, NY 10021
+1 212 585 2238

CHRISTIAN LOUBOUTIN
Paris
19 rue Jean-Jacques Rousseau
75001 Paris
+33 1 423 60531
New York
941 Madison Ave, NY 10021
+1 212 396 1884

CESARE PACIOTTI
London
11 Old Bond Street, W1S 4PX
+44 (0)20 7493 3766
Paris
12 avenue Montaigne
75008 Paris
+33 1 472 37557
Milan
Via Sant'Andrea 8
20121 Milano
+39 2 7601 3887

PRADA
New York
45 East 57th Street, NY 10022
+1 212 308 2332
London
15–16 Old Bond Street
W1S 4PS
+44 (0)20 7647 5000

SERGIO ROSSI
London
15 Old Bond Street, W1S 4PR
+44 (0)20 7629 5598
Paris
11 rue du Faubourg St Honoré
75008 Paris
+33 1 400 71089

New York
835 Madison Ave, NY 10021
+1 212 396 4814

BOTTEGA VENETA
London
33 Sloane Street, SW1X 9NR
+44 (0)20 7838 9394
Milan
Via Montenapoleone 5
20121 Milano
+39 2 7602 4495
New York
635 Madison Ave, NY 10022
+1 212 371 5511

VIVIENNE WESTWOOD
London
Westwood Studios
9–15 Elcho Street, SW11 4AU
+44 (0)20 7924 4747
New York
71 Green Street, NY 10012
+1 212 334 5200

Where to see

Bally Shoe Museum
Parkstrasse 1
5012 Schonenwerd
Zurich
Switzerland
+41 62 858 2803

Bata Shoe Museum
327 Bloor Street West
Toronto, Ontario, Canada
M58 1W7
+1 416 979 7799

The Costume Institute
Metropolitan Museum of Art
1000 Fifth Avenue
New York
NY 10028-0198 USA

Salvatore Ferragamo Museum
Palazzo Spini Feroni
Via Tornabuoni no.2
Florence
Italy
+39 5 5336 0456

Marikina Shoe Museum
(including Imelda Marcos' shoe
collection)
J. P. Rizal Street, Santa Elena
Marikina City, Manila PH, 1800
Philippines
+63 2 646 1634

Le Musée Internationale de la
    Chaussure
2 rue Sainte-Marie
26100 Romans sur Isère
France
+33 4 750 55181

Museo del Calzado
Avda de Chapi, 32
03600 Elda, Alicante
Spain
+34 965 3830 21

The Museum at the Fashion
    Institute of Technology
West 27th Street at Seventh Ave
New York, NY 10029 USA
+1 212 217 5800

Northampton Shoe Museum
Central Museum and Art Gallery
Guildhall Road
Northampton NN1 1DP
UK
+44 (0)1604 838 111

Shoe Museum
Street, Somerset, BA16 0YA
UK
+44 (0)1458 842 169

Victoria and Albert Museum
Cromwell Road
South Kensington
London SW7 2RL
UK
+44 (0)20 7942 2000

Where to surf

www.archenemys.com
www.bottegaveneta.com
www.cesarepaciotti.com
www.charlesjourdan.com
www.colinrobinson.com
www.ectomorph.com
www.fashion-heels.de
www.ferragamo.com
www.fetish-photo.com
www.ginashoes.com
www.highheelsshoemuseum.com
www.hotheels.co.uk
www.prada.com
www.sergiorossi.com
www.shoeworld.com
www.silkylegsartstudio.com
www.stantongallery.com
www.stiletto-ny.com
www.veronicas.com
www.viviennewestwood.co.uk

INDEX

ACKNOWLEDGMENTS

To my dearest sister Sarah (1958–2003)

Thanks to Emily Asquith, Sarah Rock, Hannah Barnes-Murphy, and Giulia Hetherington at Mitchell Beazley; Khalid Siddiqui, Marnie Fogg, Maggie Norden, Carol Tulloch, Liz Maclafferty, Emily Angus, Lionel and Alex Marsden, Mark Fletcher, Barbara Colombo at Cesare Paciotti, Sandra Choi and Tara Ffrench-Mullen at Jimmy Choo, Christian Louboutin, Rebecca Shawcross at Northampton Shoe Museum, Ken and Barbara Cox, Mark at Gina Shoes, Mehmet, Atlan, Attila, Aydin and Angie Kurdash, Larry Shaw, Colin Robinson, Anders Magnusson, Christian Holzknecht, Philip Castle, Terry and Liz de Havilland, Kevin Summers, Leslie Whittaker at Manolo Blahnik, Bennet Warburton, Carmen Bruegmann at Shoo, Elizabeth Greenbaum at Random House, Fabienne Brissot at Charles Jourdan, Tony at Vinmags, and Anne Muhlethaler at Christian Louboutin.

PICTURE CREDITS

5 Jimmy Choo; 6 Getty Images/Hulton Archive; 10 Bridgeman Art Library/Abbott & Holder, UK; 13 Christian Louboutin; 14 The Advertising Archives; 16 Cynthia Hampton; 19, 20 Corbis/David Lees; 24–5 Getty Images/Hulton Archive/Sasha; 26, 27 Northampton Shoe Museum; 29 Tony Armstrong-Jones © Vogue/The Condé Nast Publications Ltd; 33 Archives Sylvie Nissen/www.rene-gruau.com; 35 Corbis/Condé Nast Archive; 36 Rutledge © Vogue/The Condé Nast Publications Ltd; 37 courtesy Ken and Barbara Cox; 38 Charles Jourdan; 39 Getty Images/Hulton Archive; 40 Bridgeman Art Library/Detroit Institute of Arts, gift of W Hawkins Ferry; 41, 46-47 Getty Images/Hulton Archive; 50–1 Gina Shoes/ Mehmet Kurdash; 54 Corbis Sygma/Rick Maiman; 58 Bettmann/Corbis; 59 Skinner, Inc; 61 Vinmag Archive; 62, 64 Getty Images/Hulton Archive; 67 Skinner, Inc; 68 Mary Evans Picture Library; 71 An Idyllic Interlude by Sam Shaw, courtesy Larry Shaw/Shaw Family Archives; 74 Bettmann/Corbis; 75 courtesy Khalid Siddiqui; 76 Rex Features; 77 Corbis/John Springer Collection; 79 Corbis/Photo BDV; 80 Getty Images/Hulton Archive; 83 Mirrorpix; 84 Getty Images/Hulton Archive; 86 Gina Shoes; 87 Getty Images/Hulton Archive; 90 Guy West at Jeffrey West Shoes; 95 courtesy Khalid Siddiqui; 99 Open the box-red, Colin Robinson, www.colinrobinson.com; 100–1 Wendy Harbour/Random House Publishing; 102 Uwe Scheid Collection; 103 Northampton Shoe Museum; 105 courtesy Stanton Gallery, stanton@stantongallery.com; 108 courtesy Mikael at Silky Legs Art Studio, www.silkylegsartstudio.com; 110 Iris 6 (2001), Christian Holzknecht; 111 Northampton Shoe Museum; 113 Bridgeman Art Library/on loan to the Hamburg Kunsthalle, Germany; 114–15 YB-49 (1977), Philip Castle; 116 courtesy Marnie Fogg; 117 Terry de Havilland; 119 PYMCA/Richard Braine; 120 Kevin Summers; 122–3 Tall Order, Colin Robinson, www.colinrobinson.com; 124 Ectomorph; 127 courtesy Marnie Fogg; 128–9 Ronald Grant Archive; 130–131 PYMCA/Richard Braine; 132 Camera Press/Anthea Simms; 134 The Advertising Archives; 135 Getty Images; 136 Corbis Sygma; 138 Gina Shoes; 139 Corbis/SIN/Anthony Medley; 140 Getty Images/Lawrence Lucier; 141 Manolo Blahnik; 142 Rex Features; 143 The Advertising Archives; 144 George Ong ; 145 Jimmy Choo; 147 Getty Images/Kevin Winter; 148 left Rex Features/Ray Tang; 148-9 Chris Moore; 149 Corbis/Thierry Orban; 150-151 Rex Features; 152–5 Manolo Blahnik; 156 Terry de Havilland; 157 The Advertising Archive; 158–9 Cesare Paciotti; 161 Gina Shoes; 162–6 Christian Louboutin; 168 Anya Hindmarch; 169 Rex Features/Charles Sykes; 171 The Advertising Archives.